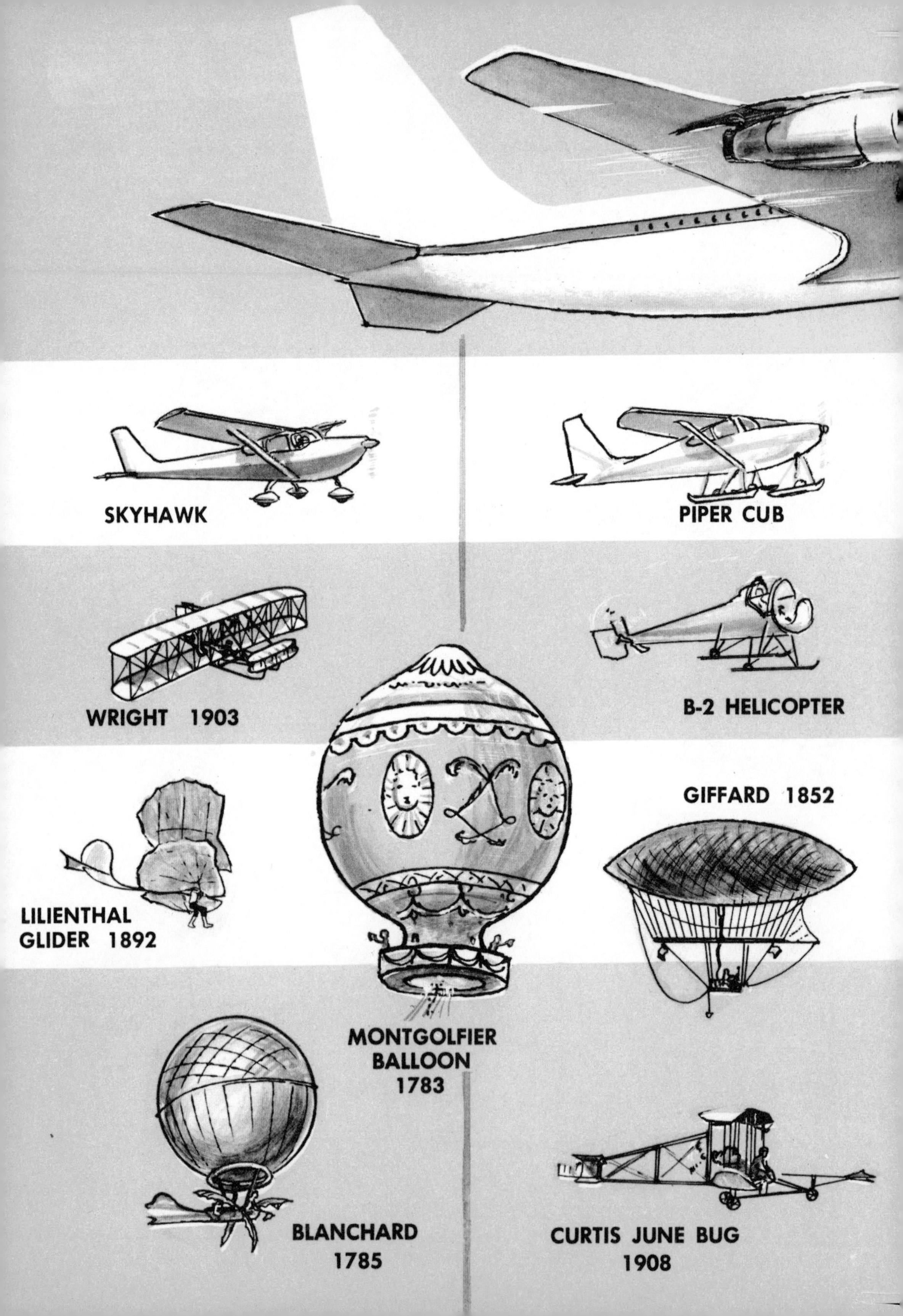
SKYHAWK
PIPER CUB
WRIGHT 1903
B-2 HELICOPTER
GIFFARD 1852
LILIENTHAL
GLIDER 1892
MONTGOLFIER
BALLOON
1783
BLANCHARD
1785
CURTIS JUNE BUG
1908

707 JET INTERCONTINENTAL
RAVEN
AG-CAT
TWIN SKYNIGHT
CHEROKEE
BONANZA
JENNY
AJ-1 WATER BOMBER

Some Other Books by Mary Elting

The Answer Book
The First Book of Nurses
The Lollypop Factory
Machines at Work
Ships at Work
Trains at Work
Trucks at Work
We Are the Government
The Helicopter Mystery *(Fiction)*
Patch *(Fiction)*
Wishes and Secrets *(Fiction)*
The Secret Story of Pueblo Bonito,
with Michael Folsom
The Story of Archeology in the Americas,
with Franklin Folsom

ACKNOWLEDGMENTS

For special help in preparing this book, the author and artists wish to thank the following: D. N. Ahnstrom of the Flight Safety Foundation, who was most generous with time, advice and anecdotes; Lycoming Division of Avco Corporation; Meteor Air Transport, Teterboro, New Jersey; Trans-World Airlines; and Morrell Gipson, our thoughtful and perceptive editor.

AIRCRAFT AT WORK

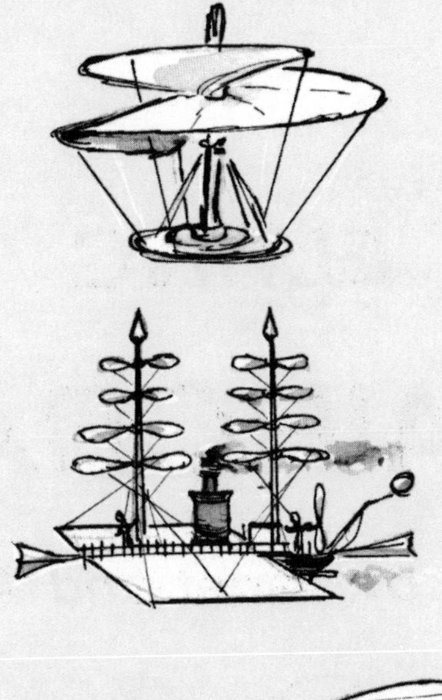

MARY ELTING

AIRCRAFT AT

Illustrated by Janet and Alex D'Amato

HARVEY HOUSE, INC.
Publishers
Irvington-on-Hudson, N.Y.

WORK

Library of Congress Catalog Number: 64-14511

Manufactured in the United States of America

HARVEY HOUSE, INC., *Publishers*
IRVINGTON-ON-HUDSON, N. Y.

KOOKIE, JACK-OF-ALL-TRADES

Kookie is an airplane. She has another name and a number, too, but the pilots at the airport call her *Kookie*.

Suppose you say to a pilot, "What kind of plane is that?"

"*Kookie*? She's a Cessna Skyhawk."

That means the Cessna Company built her, along with a lot of other planes exactly like her. All of them are called Skyhawks. (Automobiles get special names, too — Ford Thunderbirds, for instance. Or Dodge Darts or Studebaker Larks.)

A plane always has a license number, but it's not on a little license plate like an automobile plate. The number must be big, so you can see it in the sky. Some older planes have numbers painted on the wing or on the tail. But all new ones have their numbers on both sides of the body. The body is called the fuselage. *Kookie* has her number on the fuselage.

Kookie belongs to a man who runs an airport in Arizona. He owns three planes, and he calls them his fleet. One of them is something like *Kookie* — a single engine plane with one propeller in the middle of the nose. The other has two engines and propellers. It is called a twin. The twin can carry more and go faster and farther than *Kookie* can.

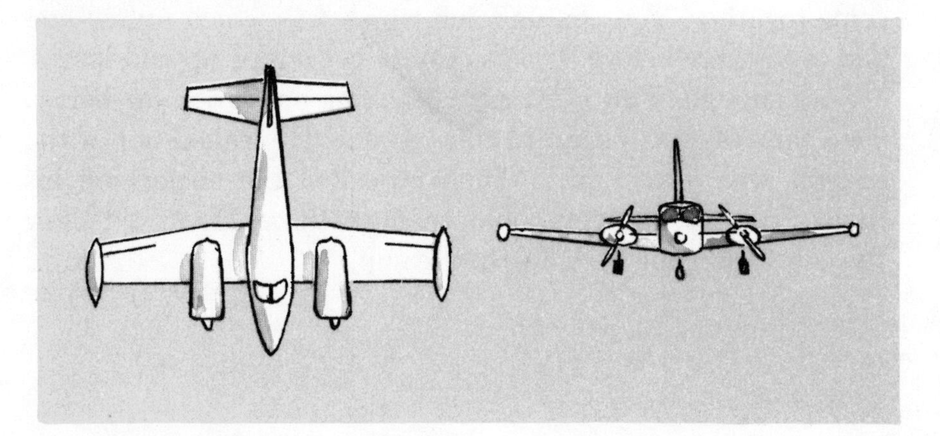

LOST AND FOUND

Joe and another pilot work for the man who runs the airport. They teach people to fly. They take passengers who want to go sightseeing. They do all kinds of flying jobs. Every day at the airport is almost always different from every other day.

One morning a Forest Ranger called Joe on the telephone.

"Two boys are lost," the Ranger said. "They went on a hike in the canyon yesterday, and they didn't come back to the campground."

"Okay," said Joe. He knew where to look. This was not the first time campers had got lost in the canyon.

Ten minutes later Joe and *Kookie* were in the air. First they made a pass over the canyon. They flew down one side of it. They flew back along the other side. Next they circled over a place where several small canyons twisted and turned and came together. You couldn't tell which was which unless you had been there before. It was easy to get mixed up and lost.

Sure enough. Two boys were standing on a rock far below. Two pairs of arms began to wave at Joe. He leaned out of the cockpit and waved back. Then he called the airport on his radio. Soon the Ranger would be down there. He would show the boys the trail back to their camp.

ODD JOBS

Joe landed at the airport and turned *Kookie* over to the line boy. A line boy is like a helper in a service station. First he topped the tank. That meant he filled *Kookie* up with gasoline. Then he wiped her windshield with a soft cloth. The windshield is made of plastic, and hard rubbing can scratch it. The line boy always works carefully. He even wears a special kind of belt buckle wrapped in soft leather so it won't scrape anything while he is working on a plane.

Joe went on into the hangar — the big building that is like a garage for planes. A man was waiting for him.

"Can you fly me across the canyon?" he asked Joe. "I left my wallet under the pillow in a motel on the other side!"

Joe knew why the man wanted to fly. There wasn't any bridge across the canyon for a long, long way. If he drove his car back to the motel, he would have to go more than two hundred miles. But as the crow flies, the motel was only a few miles from the airport.

Kookie went over and back in half an hour. And the man found his wallet.

After that, Joe had lunch. Then he flew over a new dam with a newspaper reporter who wanted to take pictures. All the way he kept having a friendly argument with the reporter who asked him to fly very low.

"No, sir!" Joe said. "It's against the law."

Next Joe took *Kookie* to the Navaho Indian Reservation. A doctor had phoned and asked to have a plane land on a certain road where a truck was parked. An Indian woman with a sick baby was waiting in the truck. Joe flew them to a hospital.

That was just about enough for one day, but Joe still had chores to do. He and the line boy rolled *Kookie* into the hangar. Next Joe pushed a button that turned on lights all around the airport. If a pilot flew in after dark, he could see where to land. Last of all Joe wound an alarm clock. The alarm would go off at midnight and turn the lights off.

But what if a pilot had to land after midnight? He would fly around above the town for a minute or two, and then the lights would go on like magic — just as soon as the town policeman heard the plane overhead! The policeman would hurry to a telephone and dial a special number. The telephone at the airport was connected with an electric switch. Instead of ringing a bell, the phone would switch on the runway lights.

FLYING CAMPERS

When Joe came to work the next morning, he saw something he'd never seen before. A little tent and a strange airplane were sitting on the grass at one side of the field.

"Hello!" Joe called.

A man and a woman came out of the tent. They were flying campers.

"We're taking a trip all around the United States," said the woman. "It's faster than automobile camping, and you see more."

"Make yourselves at home," Joe said. "We have a car you can use if you want to get groceries in town."

That is the way people almost always are around small airports.

Joe got ready for work. There was one thing he always did first. He inspected the plane he was going to use. A good pilot does this before he flies — even if he thinks everything is all right. Joe felt the propeller to be sure it had no dents in it. He kicked the tires to find out whether they had plenty of air. He made sure there were no loose wires or cables. He inspected his tank so he wouldn't run out of gas. There were more than thirty things on the check list that Joe went over carefully.

Before he finished, a small plane circled the airport. It landed and taxied to the end of the field. (When a plane travels on the ground, the pilot says it taxis.) A young man hopped out. He picked up one of the ropes that were tied to large metal rings in the ground and fastened it to a brace on his plane's wing. These tiedown ropes would keep the plane from blowing away if a sudden strong wind came up. The man was careful to make the tiedown a little bit loose. He knew that the ropes would shrink if they got wet with rain. A tight rope could shrink so much that it would break the wing.

When the man finished, he took something out of the plane. It looked like a suitcase. But it wasn't. It was a folding scooter. He unfolded it, waved to Joe and went put-putting off to sell candy to the candy stores in town.

Many flying salesmen all over the United States have scooters. They can call on more customers by plane and scooter than they can if they drive automobiles. And most airports have tiedown areas where salesmen and other visitors can park their planes.

FLYING LESSON

Two mornings a week, Joe gives flying lessons. He teaches people to pilot light planes. Most of them belong to a flying club. Some members of the club have their own planes, and they all go off together on air trips to interesting places.

One Saturday a boy named Hank came for his first lesson. He was going to be sixteen on his next birthday — old enough to get his pilot's license.

First Joe told Hank about the controls.

The *throttle* controls the flow of gasoline to the engine. More gas makes the engine go faster; less gas slows it down.

The *control column* looks like an automobile steering wheel cut in two and attached to a post. You can turn the wheel to the left or right. You can also push the whole column forward or pull it back. If you want the plane to climb, you pull it back. You push it forward if you want to point the plane's nose toward earth. A left turn on the wheel will tilt the whole plane to the left. A right turn tilts it to the right.

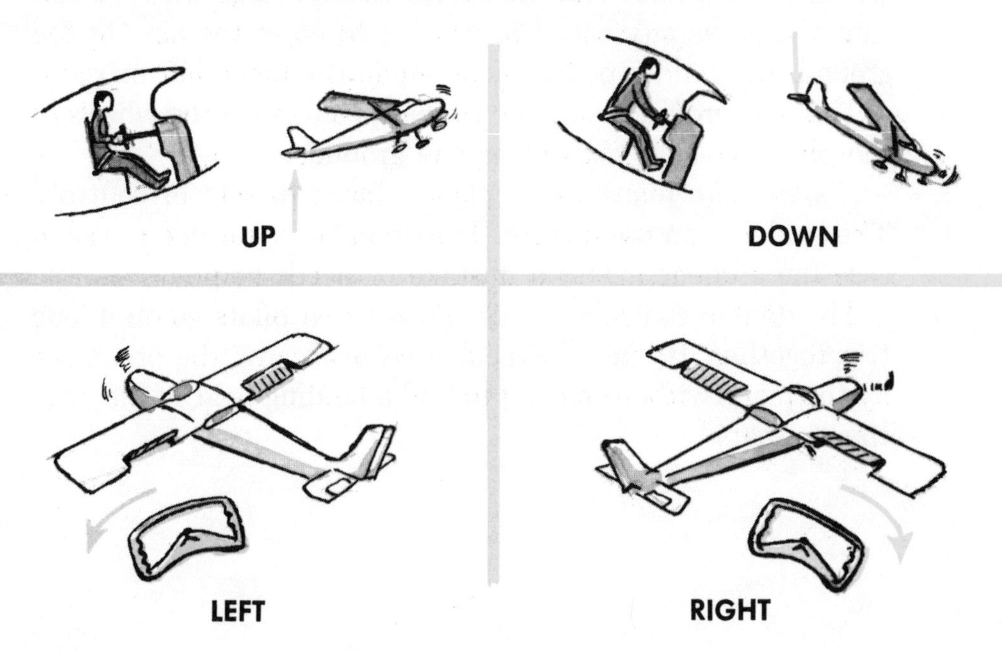

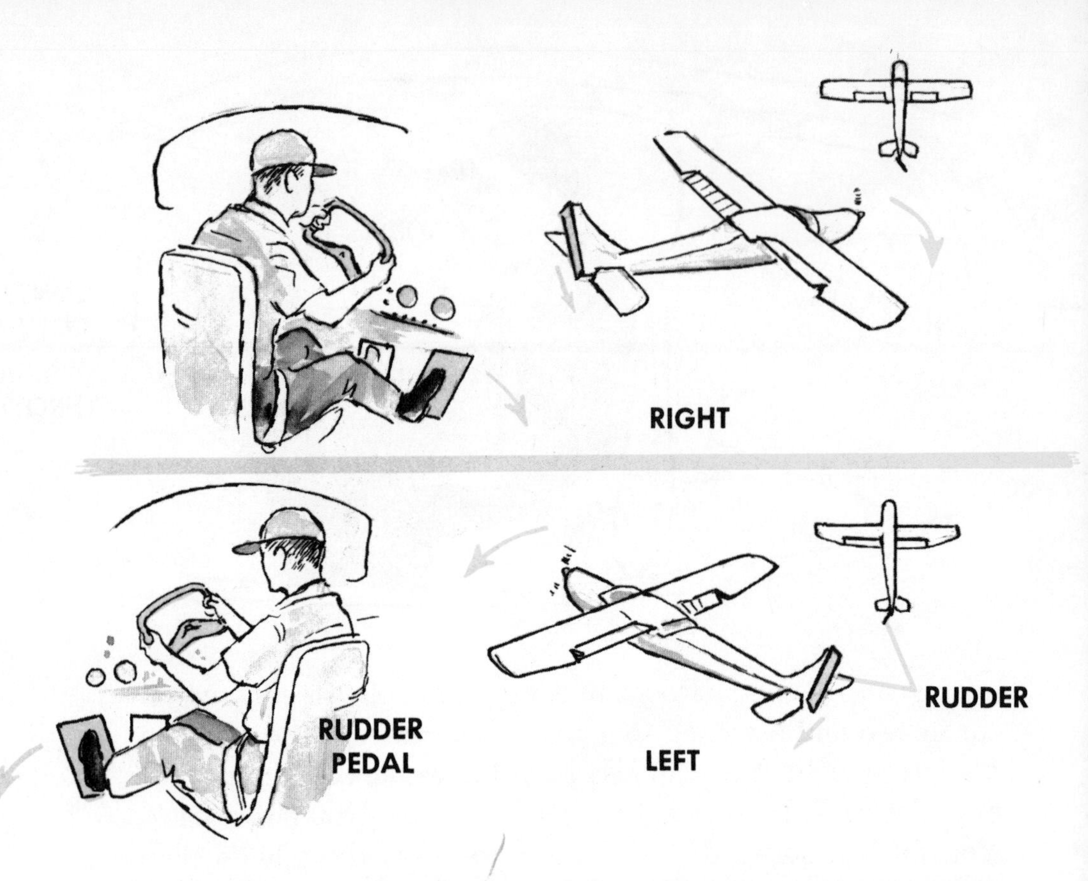

Two pedals called *rudder pedals* move the rudder in the tail. By using the pedals and the control column together, you can turn the plane any way you want it to go in the air. On the ground, the rudder pedals alone guide the plane left or right.

The *foot brakes* beside the rudder pedals slow the wheels of the plane when it taxis along the ground.

Kookie, like many other planes, has two sets of controls. The student can use one set. The other set is for Joe to use in case the student makes a mistake or needs help.

The double controls are also good when pilots go on a long trip together. If one pilot gets tired or sleepy, the other can fly the plane without having to find a landing field so they can change seats.

In the front of the cockpit are some buttons and handles and some dials that look like queer clocks. These are instruments. One is the *altimeter*. It tells how high the plane is flying. The *air speed indicator* tells how fast the plane is moving through the air.

"You'll find out more about those later. Now let's get upstairs," Joe said to Hank.

First they fastened their seat belts. Then Joe pushed the starter button and *Kookie's* propeller began to whirl. In the old days, planes didn't have starters. The pilot had to grab one of the propeller blades and give it a few hard pulls downward in order to get the engine going.

Kookie began to roll along the paved strip to the end of the field. Joe turned her around and raced back — faster, faster.

Suddenly Hank yelled, "Hey! She's getting light. She wants to fly!"

"Right!" said Joe. "Now I'm going to pull back gently on the control column."

The next moment the earth seemed to be slipping out from under and dropping away.

Kookie was airborne.

In a few minutes Hank was actually flying the plane himself. It was a wonderful feeling. He could go up or down, left or right.

"You're doing fine," Joe called out. "But don't try so hard. You'll get used to leaning with the plane when you turn — just the way you do when you ride a bike."

After a while Hank began to notice things in the world below. It was fun to see so much and so far. Best of all, he made a surprising discovery. The air felt solid under him! And *Kookie* was riding smoothly and safely through it.

When they came down, Joe showed Hank how to make a good landing. He set the main wheels down first. A moment later he eased the nose wheel down. But it was all so smooth and quick that it seemed as if the three wheels had landed at once.

HANGAR FLYING

Several pilots were talking when Hank came back to the hangar.

"Stick around a while," Joe told him. "You can find out a lot just by listening to them talk. They call it hangar flying."

One pilot said he was going to a town high in the mountains.

"Watch that runway up there," another pilot said. "It can shrink on you."

"It doesn't actually grow smaller," Joe told Hank. "It just seems to. The higher you go in the mountains, the thinner the air gets. On a hot day it is extra thin. That means a plane has to go farther and faster before it is airborne. So you have to use a longer runway. You can get a chart that tells you just what you need to know about mountain flying."

After a while Hank asked Joe, "How can they be so sure it will be good flying weather tomorrow?"

"By looking at the clouds and the weather map and listening to the radio," Joe answered. He pointed to a map that had strange marks and letters and numbers on it.

"When you learn to read this, you can tell what kind of weather is headed your way," Joe said. "We get one every day from the government. There are special broadcasts for pilots every half hour, too. We have to know a great deal about weather in order to fly safely."

ALL KINDS OF GEAR

All afternoon planes landed and took off. Hank studied them. Some had high wings like *Kookie*. Some had low wings like the twin. Some had landing gear like *Kookie's*—one wheel in front and two behind. (That is called tricycle landing gear.) Some had the single wheel under the tail. Some landing wheels folded up into the body, the way a bird's legs do when it flies. (Folding wheels are called retractable landing gear.)

In places where there is a great deal of water, some planes don't have wheels at all. They have pontoons instead. Pontoons are like unsinkable boats. They keep a plane floating when it comes down on water. People call this kind of plane a seaplane, but you're more likely to find one on a lake or river or bay than on the open sea where the waves are high.

In wilderness country, seaplanes often take the place of cars and railroads. Men go hunting or fishing by plane to save themselves long trips on foot or in a canoe. But they still take along a paddle or two, just in case of engine trouble far from shore. They can sit astride the pontoons and paddle the plane in to land.

An amphibian is a plane that can come down on either land or water.

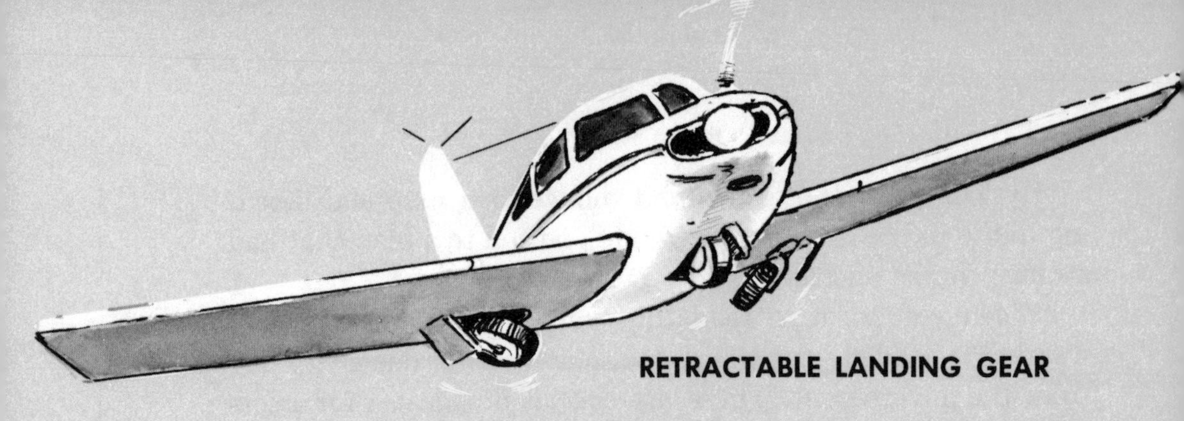

RETRACTABLE LANDING GEAR

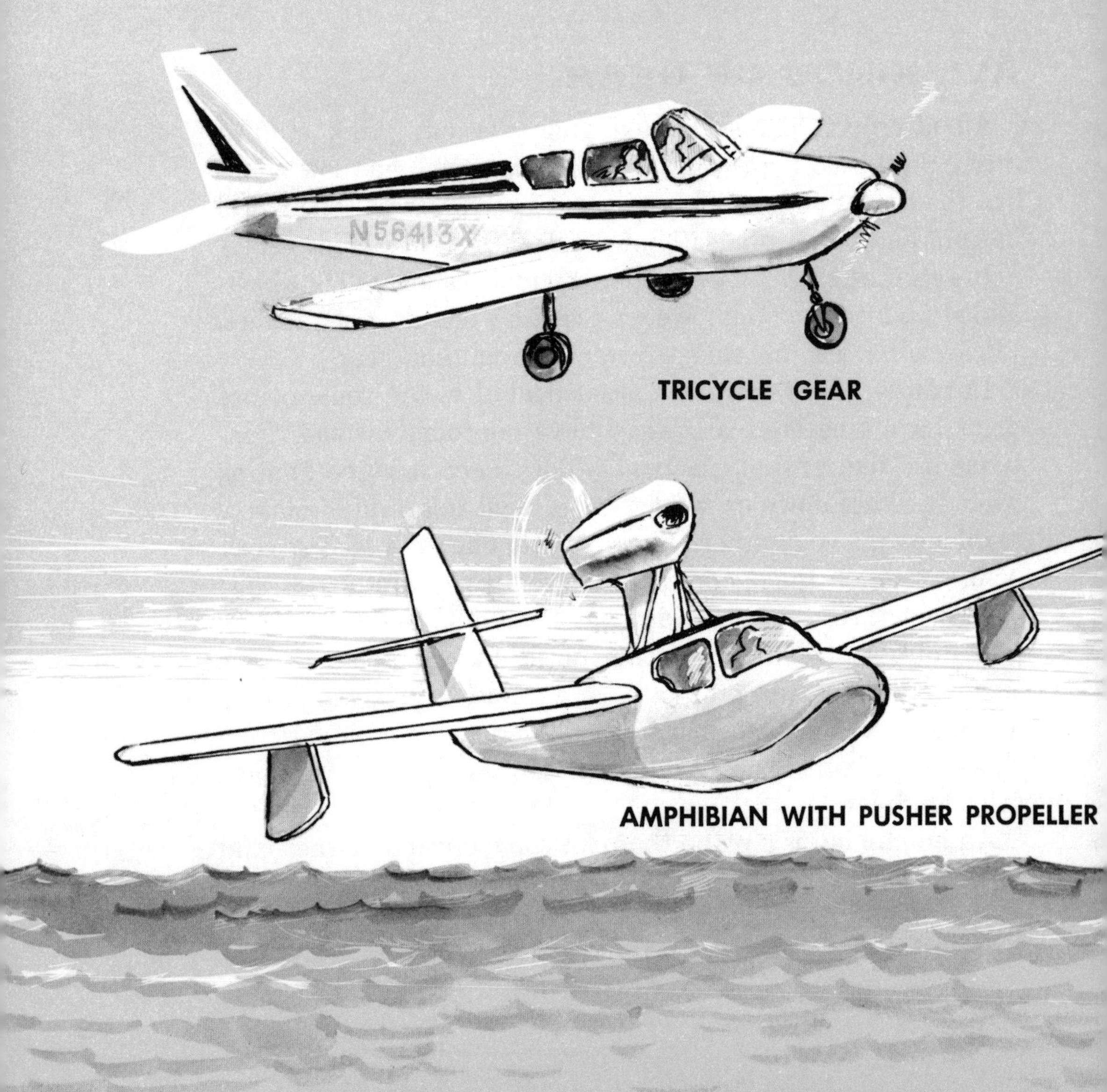

TRICYCLE GEAR

AMPHIBIAN WITH PUSHER PROPELLER

CONVENTIONAL GEAR

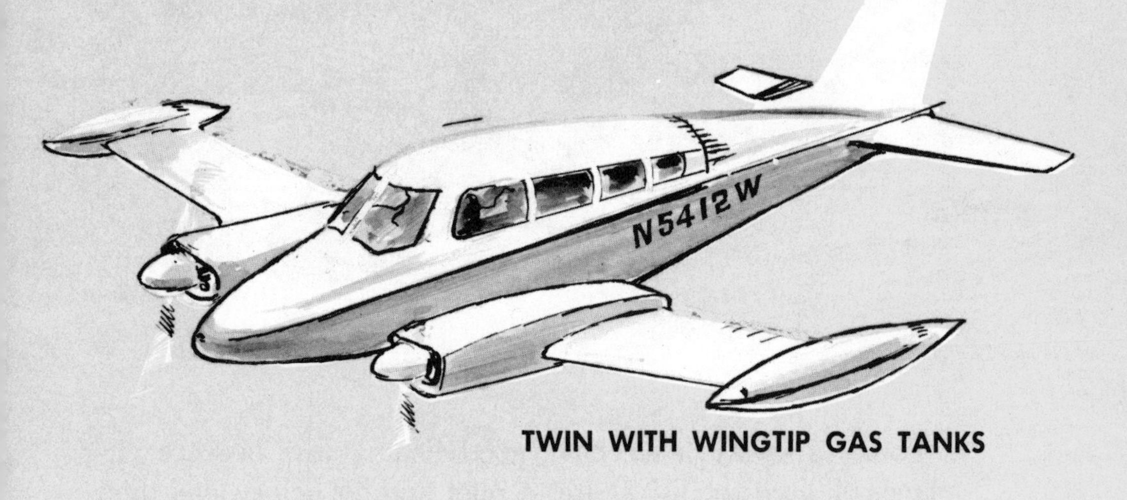

TWIN WITH WINGTIP GAS TANKS

SEAPLANE WITH PONTOONS

Some far-away lakes have good fishing just because air-planes planted the fish there! A pilot and his helper load their plane with big milk cans full of water and baby fish. Then they fly in low and empty the cans into the lake.

The planting planes belong to the government's Fish and Wildlife Service. Sometimes they plant beaver. Men catch the beaver in places where there are too many. Then the pilot takes them high up in the mountains where they can build dams that will help stop floods. Each beaver rides in a little cage attached to a parachute. When it touches the earth, the cage opens automatically and lets the beaver out.

For winter flying, a plane can have skis instead of wheels or pontoons. The skis slip along over snow or ice, and the plane can easily land or take off.

When snow gets very deep in high mountains, wild animals are likely to starve. So government planes, with skis for emergency landings, fly over herds of elk or deer and drop hay to them. In bad winters, they drop hay to cattle on ranches, too.

Pilots have skis on their planes when they do winter bush-hopping in Alaska. Bush-hopping is flying in wilderness country where it is a long way between towns. In many places there are no roads, even in summer. Bush-hoppers bring people food and mail and medicine and movies and friends.

The members of a flying club in Europe are also mountain climbers. They put skis on their planes so they can land high on glaciers. From there they go up the peaks on foot.

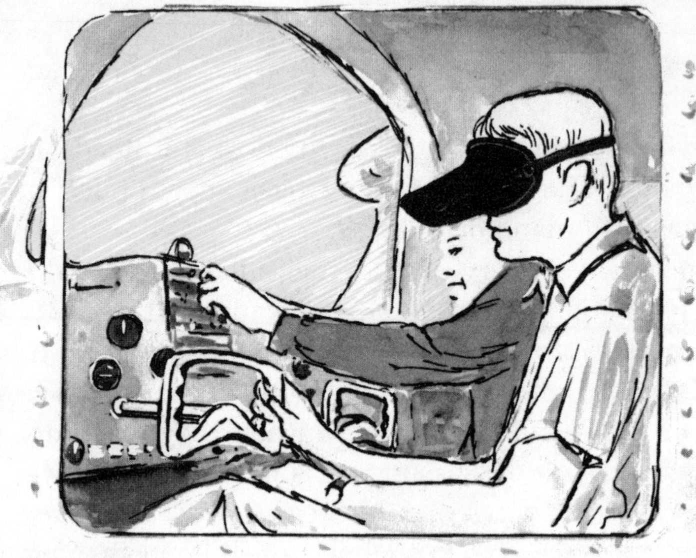

SOLO

You have to be a very good pilot to do bush-hopping and glacier landing. For some difficult jobs you need a special license. But you can start out with just an ordinary one. This is how you get it:

First you fly with your teacher. That is called dual flight. Then you fly solo — that is, alone. You must have at least 35 hours of combined dual and solo time in the air around an airport. Then you must learn to fly across country. For this you must use a special aviation map that tells you where airports are. The map shows mountains and towers and other dangers to avoid.

You must also learn to use a compass and other instruments that can guide you when it is too dark or cloudy to see the earth.

The teacher has a gadget called a hood that makes these instrument lessons very real. The hood covers your head and face. It has little peepholes that let you see the instruments in front of you. Everything else is invisible, the way it would be in a fog.

You put on the hood, and the teacher tells you to turn the plane around and fly in the opposite direction. You must watch the compass all the time in order to know when you are headed east instead of west, or south instead of north. It is hard to turn when you can't see the ground. You may get dizzy at first. But soon you learn just to look at the instruments and quit thinking about anything else.

After all this, you take a written examination. A man from the Federal Aviation Agency gives you a flight test. A doctor gives you a medical examination. If you pass, your teacher has the right to snip a piece off your shirttail and say "Hooray! I boosted another pilot into the sky!"

THE CAP

Many pilots all over the country belong to an organization called the Civil Air Patrol — CAP for short. They do volunteer rescue work of many kinds.

Once an earthquake in California wrecked a town. Telephone wires were down and the radio station was knocked out. Civil Air Patrol pilots immediately flew in with doctors, nurses, Red Cross workers and supplies. They used their plane radios to keep the town in touch with the outside world.

CAP pilots search for people who get lost. Once they found a hunter who had been wandering for days in the Maine woods. Another time they saved a prospector lost in the mountains. They locate children who have wandered away from picnics.

In many places the CAP has classes for boys and girls who want to learn how to fly.

I FOLLOW ROADS

When a pilot looks at the ground below and follows a map, he calls it VFR flying. That means he flies according to *V*isual *F*light *R*ules.

At night pilots watch for lights that help them locate towns and cities, roads and airports shown on their maps. Beacon lights of different kinds tell them where they are.

Pilots who do a lot of flying in cloudy, foggy country have special scientific instruments. These instruments use radio beams to help tell the pilot where he is and guide him down through clouds or darkness. When he follows *I*nstrument *F*light *R*ules he calls it IFR flying.

In the old days there were no special aviation maps and no radio. Pilots said they flew by the seat of the pants. One old-fashioned pilot still prefers to use a highway map. He says he does IFR flying — that is, "*I F*ollow *R*oads."

SPRAYERS AND DUSTERS

Pilots all over the country fly crop spraying planes. They must have special licenses. This is the most dangerous kind of work, and it takes great skill.

Before the pilot goes to work, he walks around the farm and studies it. He looks for telephone wires and power lines and trees that border the fields. The plane will be flying low, and he doesn't want to bump into anything. He wonders about the wind. When it is too strong, it will blow the spray where he doesn't want it to go. How can he tell? He lights a wooden kitchen match. If the wind blows the match out, then it's no day for spraying.

The pilot puts on a gas mask and a special suit that protects his skin. The spray is meant to poison bugs, but it can also poison a flier. Then he swoops in very low over the field, so that the chemical will hit the spot it's supposed to hit. A special pump squirts the spray out of a tank and down through nozzles underneath the plane.

Sometimes a farmer wants his field dusted instead of sprayed. One plane in Georgia or Mississippi can dust more cotton in one day than a hundred machines pulled by tractors on the ground. At harvest time, the duster spreads a chemical that makes leaves fall off the cotton plants. This speeds the work of picking the cotton.

Almost any kind of plane can do spraying and dusting. But one, called the Ag-Cat, is specially built for the job. It is a biplane. That means it has two wings, one above the other. A biplane can fly more safely at low speeds than a single-wing plane.

With different kinds of chemicals, the duster and sprayer planes protect orange and lemon orchards, grain fields, and many kinds of vegetables.

In rice-growing country in Arkansas, planes do almost all of the work except harvesting. First they drop the seeds. Then they spray chemicals that kill weeds without harming the rice plants. Later they spread fertilizer. As the plants grow, the planes still have work to do. They fly around scaring off ducks and geese that like to eat the tender young rice shoots.

FLYING FARMERS

An airplane is a real farm tool. If a grasshopper plague starts, pilots can stop it by dropping poisoned bran for the grasshoppers to eat. Farmers often fly over big fields and judge by the color they see how well the plants are growing. In ranch country, pilots drop chemicals that kill useless brush that is taking the place of grass on cattle ranges.

A flying farmer can leave the North in the morning, buy tomato plants in the South at noon, come back and have the plants all set out in his field by night. He can pick up baby chickens and fly them home. He can rush to the factory for parts when his tractor breaks down. Ranchers use planes to look for stray cattle.

Many farmers belong to flying farmer clubs. They take trips together when the work's all done in the fall.

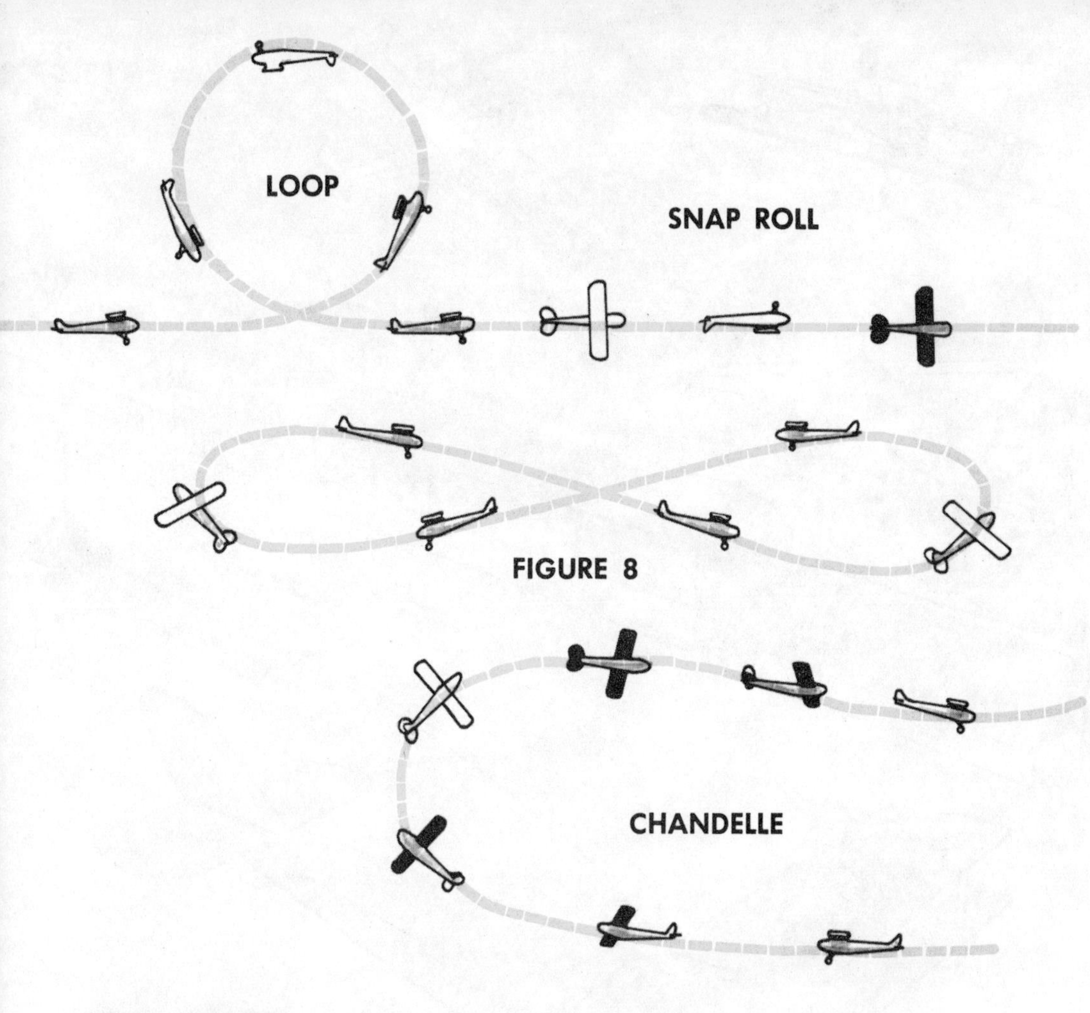

STUNTS

One flying farmer is different. He works six days a week in his fields. But on Sundays, in good weather, he does aerobatics. That means he does stunts with his plane in the air, the way an acrobat performs in a circus.

He starts out early in the morning. The air is calm then, and traffic hasn't begun to move around the airport. For half an hour he does loops and snap rolls, lazy 8's and Chandelles. For some of his stunts he stays high in the air. For others he says he flies only "two hundred feet above the deck."

Years ago, he used to do tricks so close to the ground that his wing almost touched the earth. But safety rules make him keep higher in the air now. In the days when planes were an unusual sight, stunt pilots went all around the country with flying circuses. Men climbed from the wing of one plane to the wing of another in mid-air! Women did, too. They hung by their feet from rope ladders. They pretended to have fights on the upper wings of biplanes. It was part of the act for one man to get knocked off. But he always saved himself at the last moment by opening a parachute. Some pilots even crashed old planes into trees on purpose, just to give the audience a shock.

Many of the daredevil fliers were killed. Sometimes a few onlookers got hurt. That's why flying circuses have gone out of fashion. But there are still air shows where skillful pilots do wonderful stunts with their planes.

The flying farmer practices at his home airport, so he'll be ready when the big shows come along.

SIGNS IN THE SKY

At airports near the seashore, a pilot sometimes has a banner-towing job. The banner is made of huge letters cut out of canvas and fastened together with rope. When you see the letters stretched out behind a plane, they spell words — like BASEBALL TONIGHT.

Men at the airport lay the banner on a runway. The last letter has a big loop of rope on it. Two men open the loop and hold it on poles high above their heads. Now the towing plane swoops down toward them. It catches the loop with a hook dangling from a rope under the fuselage. As the hook grabs the loop, the pilot puts the plane into a steep climb and whips the sign up from the runway. Off he goes toward the seashore where people on the beaches will look at the sign all day long. For safety he isn't allowed to tow it over cities or places where it might get in the way of other planes.

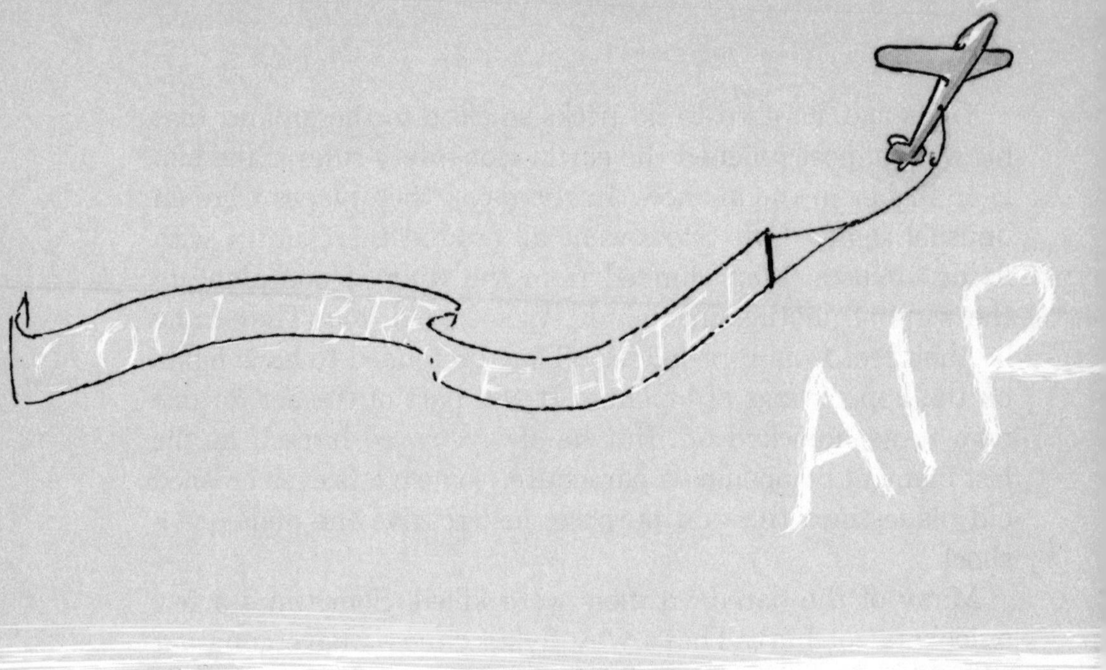

Skywriting is the opposite of banner-towing. You see it most often in the air over cities. A skywriting pilot makes words with smoke. He has to write the letters backwards, just the way a sign painter does when he puts letters on the inside of a window. But the pilot can't rub out any mistakes he makes! The pilot sits in the open cockpit of his plane, with a board on his lap. Fastened to the board is a drawing of what he is going to write. For each letter he has instructions that

tell him when to fly straight and for how long, when to turn and how much.

The smoke for writing comes from stuff like castor oil that pours out in a white cloud when the engine's exhaust heats it. Chemicals added to the oil can make colored smoke.

Once a pilot was supposed to write AIR SHOW over New York. He made a mistake, and it came out AIR SOW. Everybody joked about the skywriter who couldn't spell, but the mistake was good for business. More people came to the show than ever before.

A new kind of skywriting is called skytyping. A machine automatically lets out puffs of smoke to form the letters. The machine is run by a kind of mechanical brain that tells it when to puff out which letter. The planes that carry the machines are swift, old-fashioned fighters left over from the war.

RAINMAKING AND HURRICANE BUSTING

In some places pilots have tried to bring rain in very dry weather. Rainmaking is called cloud-seeding. The pilot flies above a cloud and sprinkles it with "seeds" of dry ice. Or he may spray out a special kind of chemical. Snowflakes or raindrops sometimes do form around the seeds. But they don't always fall where moisture is needed.

The United States Weather Bureau is doing experiments with cloud-seeding. Perhaps seeds can make rain in the great whirling clouds that form during a hurricane. If this rain can be made to fall in the ocean, maybe the hurricane can be stopped before it hits land.

One big Weather Bureau plane has often flown straight into a hurricane off the Florida coast to find out more about storms. Men in the plane use instruments that measure the speed of the terrible winds. They record wind direction and air temperature. All of this will help scientists to understand storms. Perhaps someday they will be able to control hurricanes and tornadoes.

FLYING SCIENTISTS

Scientists use planes in many ways. They explore jungles from the air. Sometimes they discover ancient hidden cities where nobody has lived for hundreds of years. Scientists fly over the North Pole and the South Pole. Planes have helped them to find out a great deal about the Arctic Ocean and the continent of Antarctica. The mountains near the South Pole are so high and so cold that no one could ever visit them on foot. But pilots can take pictures of them.

A pilot can also work with scientists hunting for new mines. They use a gadget called a magnetometer that hangs at the end of a long wire underneath the plane. If the pilot flies over a place where there is a certain kind of iron ore in the earth, the magnetometer helps to locate it.

In Canada a great mountain of iron ore was once discovered far from a railroad. The mining men asked a pilot for help. They wanted him to find out quickly where to build a new railroad through the wilderness. In the old days, it would have taken months, maybe years, for men on foot to discover the easiest way to cross that wild country. The pilot and his helpers finished the whole search in one summer. They just took good, clear photographs. The pictures told the experts where to lay the rails.

Aerial photographs tell engineers where the best place is for a dam. Air scouts help lumber companies to locate trees the right size for cutting. Flying tree-doctors help to keep the forests healthy and growing. On a forest scouting expedition, the scientist looks out for insects that destroy trees. He doesn't have to catch a single one of them. He can tell by the color of the leaves whether bugs are at work in the forest below. If he spots trouble, a duster pilot goes out to kill the pests.

Pilots who fly over mountain forests have to know about winds and air currents. A current that is rising toward the top

of a mountain does no harm. But one that falls swiftly downward can dash a plane to the ground.

GLIDERS

The pilots who know most about currents are those who fly gliders. A glider is an airplane that has no engine. It has to be launched with a push or a pull that sends it into the air. Then the pilot keeps it aloft by steering it into rising air.

A good glider pilot can soar for many hours and travel a great distance — as much as 400 miles without landing.

The secret of glider flight is this: When the sun heats the earth, bubbles of warm air form. A bubble gets bigger and bigger and finally starts to rise — the way bubbles do when you heat a pot of water. This rising air is called a thermal. The pilot knows where to look for thermals. He steers his glider into them, one after another, and the rising air keeps him up.

Air currents go up over warm earth . . . come down over woods . . . go up over towns . . . come down over lakes . . .

Gliders are also called sailplanes. They are so light, and they can come down so gently, that they don't need regular landing gear. Just one wheel can be enough.

People fly gliders mostly for fun now, but men were once very serious about them. Experiments with gliders helped inventors to understand flight. Then they could go ahead and build planes with engines.

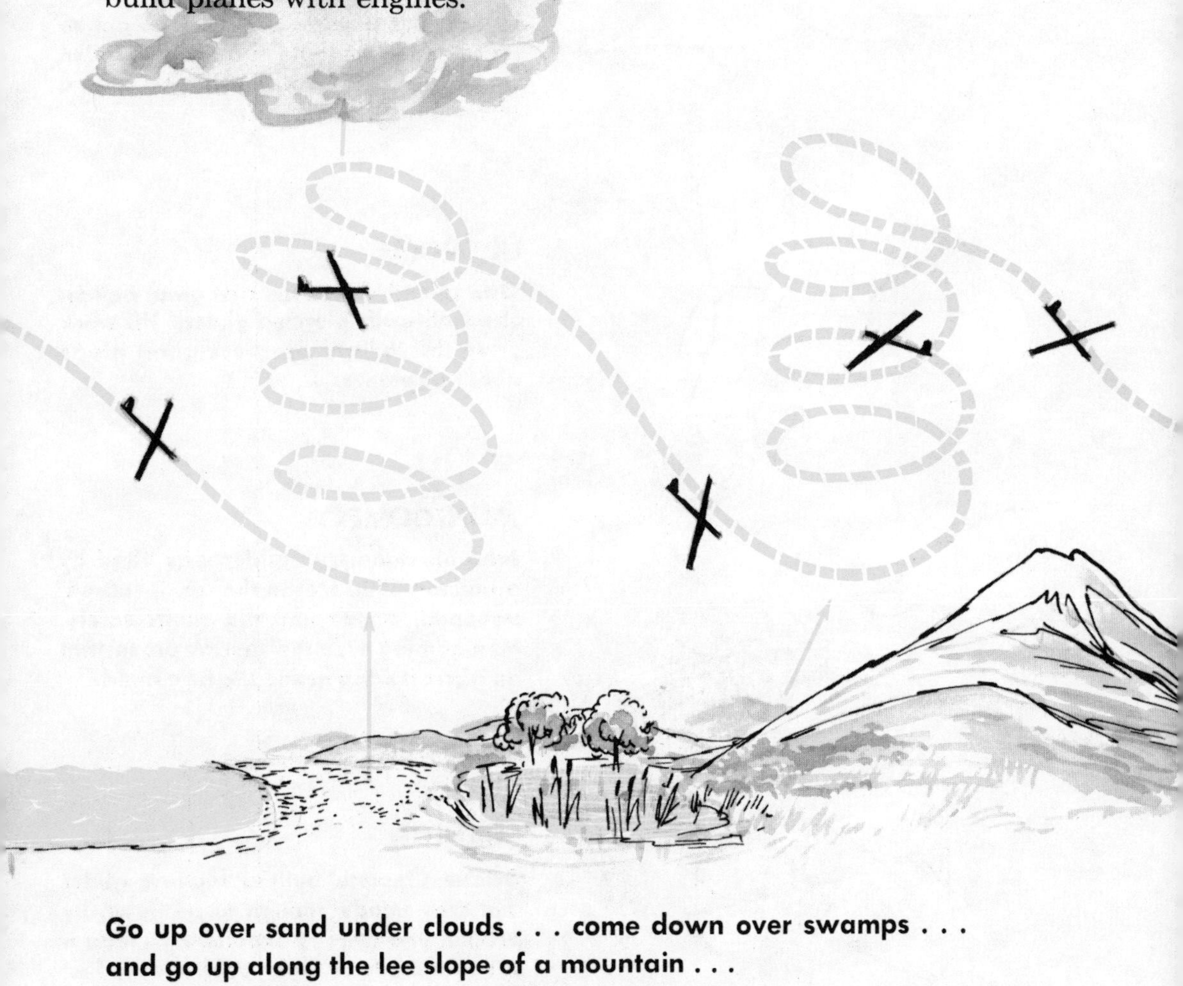

Go up over sand under clouds . . . come down over swamps . . . and go up along the lee slope of a mountain . . .

GLIDERS

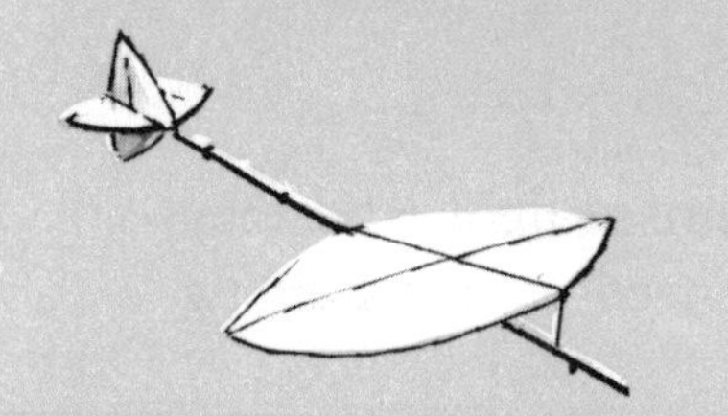

CAYLEY

Sir George Cayley built models like this one before he made a big glider that actually flew. Cayley invented the first rudders for aircraft.

LE BRIS' ALBATROSS

Le Bris was a ship's captain who got so interested in the flight of a sea bird called an albatross that he built and flew a glider named for the bird.

LILIENTHAL

Otto Lilienthal was the first great builder of scientifically planned gliders. His work gave the Wright brothers good ideas about airplanes.

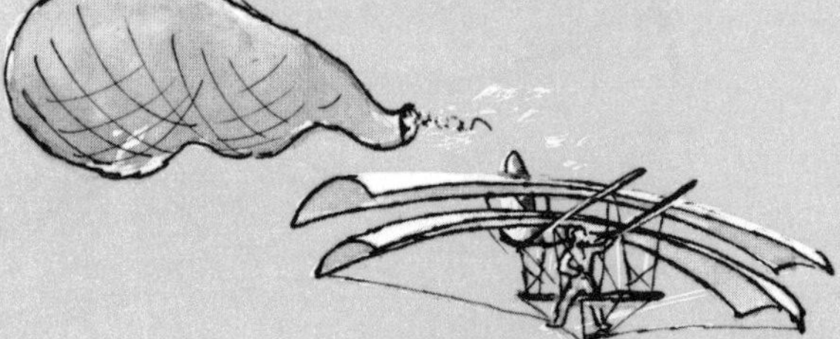

MONTGOMERY

John Montgomery's glider was lifted by a balloon 3500 feet in the air. It soared, swooped, circled and did stunts safely. Montgomery was the first to prove that an aircraft wing needed to be curved.

CHANUTE

Octave Chanute built a biplane glider that was steady enough to be flown by people who weren't experts. He made a scientific study of flight, and was the first to predict that gliding would someday become a sport.

POWERED AIRCRAFT

WRIGHT BROTHERS

This is the first successful Wright machine. It made four flights before it crashed. The Wrights never used the name airplane. They called all of their craft Wright Flyers.

LANGLEY

Samuel Langley made many experiments with flying machines, but he always had very bad luck. His plane, called an aerodrome, was not successfully flown till 1914, eight years after he died.

SANTOS-DUMONT

Alberto Santos-Dumont built biplanes that were like box kites joined together and driven by an engine. They could fly only a few hundred feet.

BLERIOT

After eight years of experimenting, Louis Bleriot built the first powered monoplane ever to make a successful flight. In 1908 it stayed up 8½ minutes.

CURTISS' JUNE BUG

Glenn Curtiss made a speed record in 1908 with the June Bug. It flew thirty-nine miles an hour and won a prize.

LEVAVASSEUR'S ANTOINETTE

This long, thin monoplane was called the Antoinette by its designer Levavasseur. An Antoinette almost succeeded in flying from France to England in 1909, but its engine stopped, and the plane was the first to make a safe forced landing on water.

The first man to fly a glider was probably Giovanni Battista Danti. He lived in Italy about five hundred years ago. Science and mathematics and flying all interested him. But Danti had to give up his experiments with wings because people called him a wicked magician. They said he was doing the work of the devil, so they burned his glider and made him leave Italy.

Then about a hundred and fifty years ago, men began to discover they could build machines that had engines and wheels. Soon steam engines were running trains and paddle wheel steamships. Inventors began to dream of machines that would carry them into the air. They built more and better gliders. Someday, they were sure, they would have planes good enough to fly and engines light enough to move them. Gasoline engines, which were much lighter than steam engines, brought the day nearer.

Orville and Wilbur Wright built a glider and flew it. They also studied engines. Finally they found the right combination of wings and power. They made the first successful flight on December 17, 1903, at Kitty Hawk, North Carolina. Nobody thought the Wright brothers were doing the work of the devil. In fact, the exact place where their plane took off was known as Kill Devil Hill!

BALLOONS AND BLIMPS

Airplanes are called heavier-than-air-craft. Balloons are lighter-than-air-craft. Balloons carried men up above the earth long before gliders did. The first one was filled with hot air. Later, balloonists used a very light gas called hydrogen. Men who belong to balloon clubs today use the kind of gas that you have in your kitchen for cooking. Of course, it is dangerous. A spark of fire or lightning can make it explode. But the club members are very careful, and they fly only on clear days.

The balloon is a huge rubber bag covered with a net made of rope. At the bottom of the net hangs a basket with seats for several passengers. When the bag has been filled with gas, it lifts net, basket and people into the air. The wind blows the balloon from place to place.

When it's time to land, the pilot pulls on a special rope. This opens a valve in the balloon and gas begins to spill out. With less and less gas, the balloon sinks slowly to earth. Of course, the pilot tries to choose a soft field for a landing!

Scientists use balloons, too. They put a telescope into the basket and send it high above the clouds. A camera attached to the telescope takes pictures of the moon and the stars. The pictures are very clear, because there is not much smoke or dust so far above the earth.

The gas that lifts this kind of balloon does not burn. It is called helium. (Balloon clubs don't use it because it is too expensive.)

There is no way to steer an ordinary round balloon. But suppose you made the gas bag in the shape of a cigar and put an engine and propeller and a rudder on the basket. This kind of aircraft goes where you want it to go, and it is called a dirigible or an airship or a blimp.

Radiosonde balloons are tracked by radar. They send back information on weather. A parachute below the balloon lowers instruments gently.

Dirigibles once flew passengers regularly across the Atlantic Ocean and even around the world. The dangerous hydrogen gas worked well for a while. But one day something happened, and the whole airship caught fire. Many passengers were killed. After that, people didn't want to ride in dirigibles.

American Army and Navy blimps filled with helium have been used for gathering information about the weather. One double blimp, called a Vee-Balloon, carries scientific instruments that are being tested in the air. This blimp's odd shape makes it very steady, even in rough weather.

A dirigible flies much more slowly than a plane. Since most people nowadays want to go from place to place in a great hurry, they wouldn't travel by airship, even if it was filled with safe helium. But they might like to take long vacation cruises in a very fancy one. A dirigible with an atomic engine could fly around the world without ever landing to get fuel. Passengers could get on and off along the way. They would come and go by shuttle plane. A hook dangling from the airship would catch the plane and pull it close for loading and unloading.

The atomic dirigible hasn't been built yet, but men may try it one of these days. It would be an exciting experiment.

HELICOPTERS

DA VINCI

Leonardo da Vinci more than four hundred years ago invented a helicopter that would have worked if he had had an engine to run it.

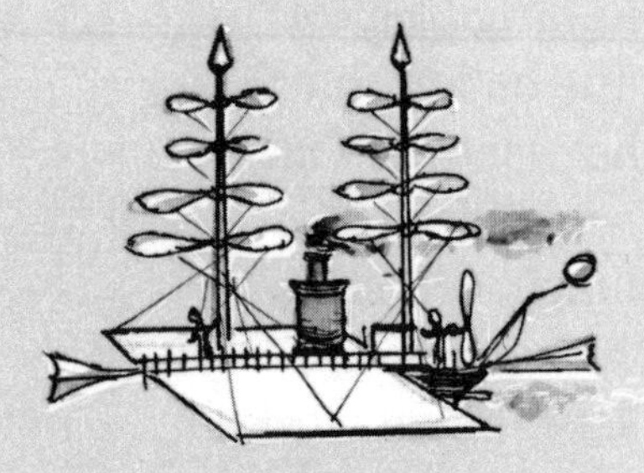

DE LA LANDELLE

De la Landelle, who dreamed up this idea for a steam-driven helicopter, built other more practical models, but did not succeed in flying them. He also invented the word aviation.

CAYLEY

Sir George Cayley built several toy helicopters that had clock-works for engines. One model rose 90 feet into the air.

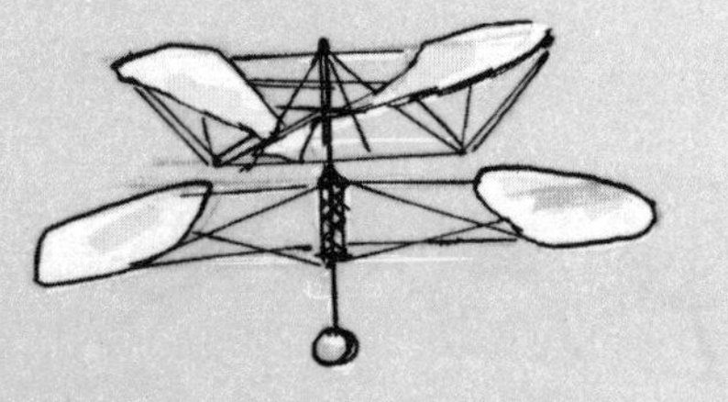

FORLANINI

Enrico Forlanini's model copter was run by steam. Since an engine to make the steam was too heavy, he heated the boiler over a flame and then attached it to the machine which could fly for about 20 seconds.

SIKORSKY

Igor Sikorsky began building copters when he was a boy and kept at it until he had invented some of the world's best and most useful whirlybirds.

BALLOONS AND SUCH

DE GUSMAO

Before balloons were invented, a monk named De Gusmao seriously proposed this silly machine which was supposed to lift itself by magnets.

STEPHEN & JOSEPH MONTGOLFIER

The Montgolfier brothers built balloons that flew because they were filled with hot air. Since hot air is lighter than cold, it can rise and carry a balloon up.

BLANCHARD & JEFFRIES

This balloon carried the first pilot (Blanchard) and passenger (Jeffries) from France to England. The balloon was filled with hydrogen gas.

GIFFARD

Henri Giffard built the first airship that could be navigated. The bag was filled with hydrogen. A steam engine gave it power, and a rudder guided it.

PICCARD

Auguste Piccard made many scientific flights in a modern balloon that carried him higher above the earth than anyone had ever gone before.

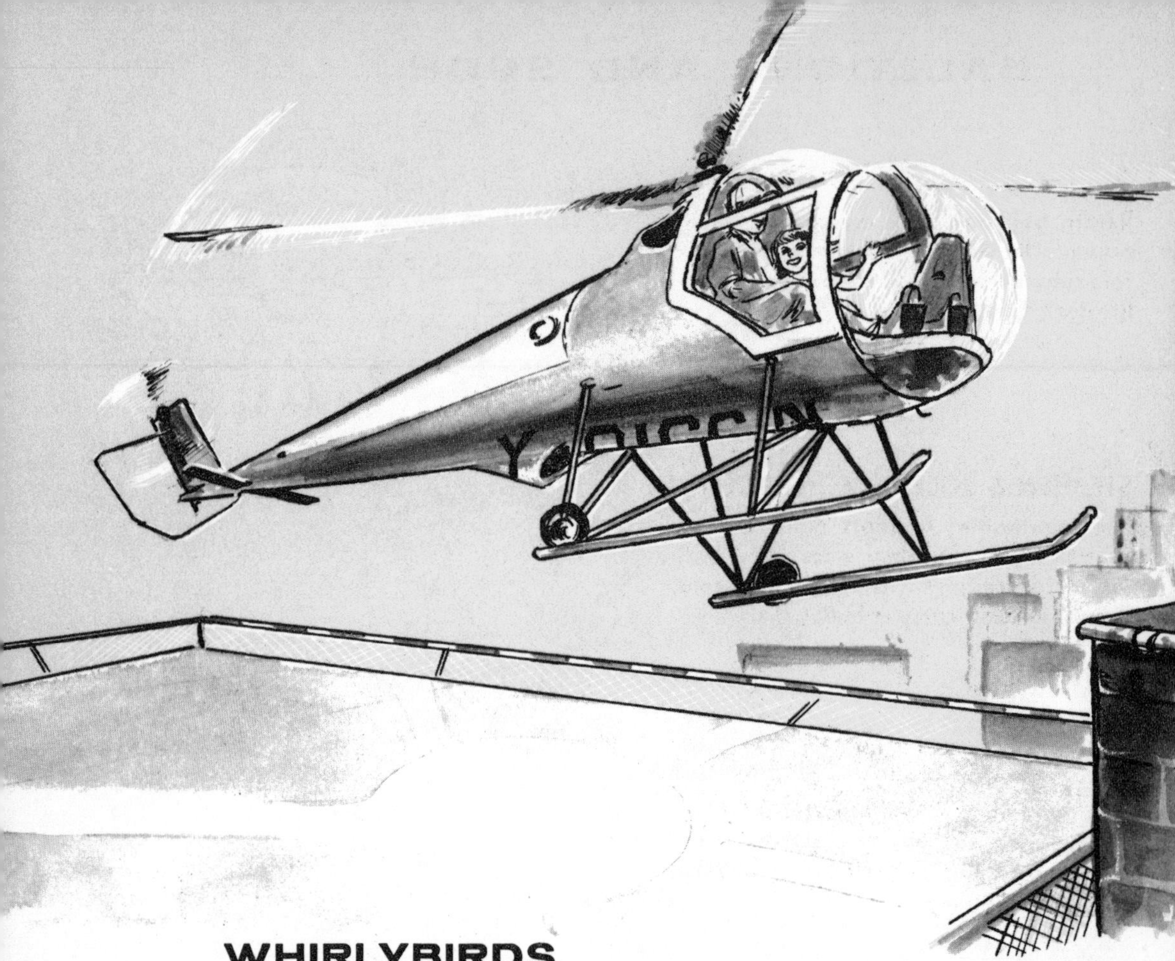

WHIRLYBIRDS

A helicopter is an aircraft with whirling wings. Pilots call it a whirlybird or a chopper. The long blades, called rotors, go round and round like a propeller on its back, but they really lift the copter just the way a fixed wing does.

The wonderful thing about rotors is that they can take the copter almost straight up from the ground and bring it back almost straight down. They can make it fly backward as well as forward. Or they can keep it hovering above one spot. This means that a helicopter needs no long runway for landing or taking off. A space just a little wider than its rotors is usually enough.

The idea for the helicopter probably came from a toy. Long ago the Chinese made tiny toy rotors that flew when they were whirled swiftly by hand. The Wright brothers had one of these Chinese rotors, and they studied it carefully. Later, many inventors tried to build copters, but they had a hard time making them safe enough and easy enough to operate.

One problem was this: The copter's body wouldn't stay put. It whirled in one direction, while the rotors whirled in the opposite direction. To keep the body from spinning, engineers put a small propeller in the tail. It does not push the copter through the air. It just keeps the machine steady.

Some choppers have two sets of rotors that whirl in opposite directions. With this arrangement the body doesn't turn.

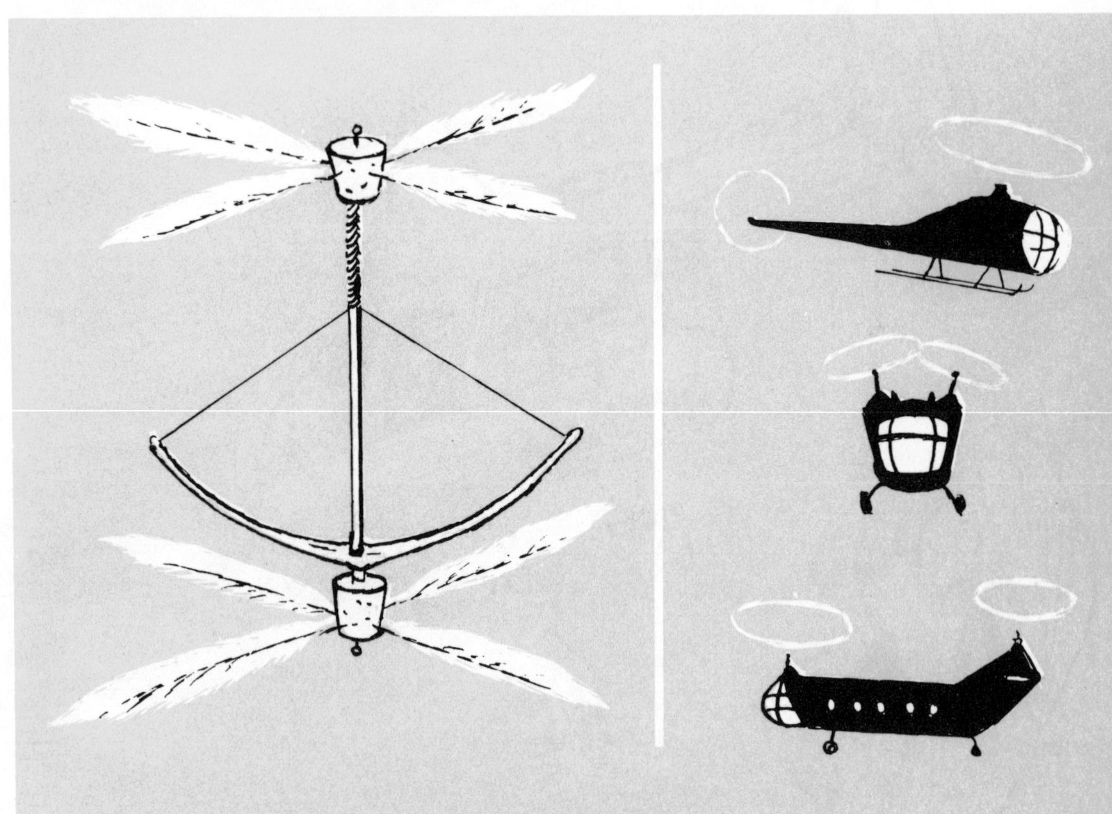

Copters are still not easy to fly. But they can do such wonderful things that people use them more and more. Almost every day a pilot rescues someone with his chopper. For instance, some boys tried to climb a high cliff and got stuck halfway to the top. They couldn't go on up, and they were afraid to climb down. A copter pilot flew up and hovered close to the cliff, while a crewman tossed out a rescue harness. One by one the boys put on the harness, and the crewman hoisted them aboard.

A copter can hoist people off wrecked boats or floating ice or the roof of a burning building. A firefighting copter carries a tank full of chemicals that it can drop to smother a blaze.

Copters fly along beside electric power lines to make sure the wires are all right. They go back and forth above cross-country oil and gas pipes looking for leaks. They do crop dusting much more safely than a plane can, because they can fly slowly close to the ground, and they have no trouble hopping over telephone wires and trees.

In Florida copters protect the farmer's crops in cold weather. The whirling rotors keep air moving over a field. They stir the warmer upper air down into the cold air near the ground, and this often keeps fruit and vegetables from freezing. After a rain, the rotors fan moisture away so that fruit and berries can be picked before they spoil.

Cowboys in copters track down cattle that get lost during snowstorms. They look out for broken fences and carry supplies to other cowboys out on the range. The Texas Rangers have a copter. Once in a while they use it to search for rustlers who have stolen cattle.

One helicopter swings a skull-cracker. That is a huge steel ball that breaks down the walls of old buildings so that new buildings can be put up. The ball hangs at the end of a long steel cable underneath the copter. The pilot hovers high above the building and sways his machine gently until the ball begins to swing back and forth far below. Soon it swings into the wall and knocks the bricks down.

Other copters help to put buildings up. They hoist big pieces of wood and steel. They can even lift up a steeple that has been built on the ground and set it in place on top of a new church.

It often happens that oil well drillers have to work in the middle of a swamp or on platforms built in the ocean far from shore. Helicopters with pontoons bring food and tools and machine parts, and they often carry men to and from work.

Big helicopters carry passengers from one airport to another. Most airports are quite a long way from the centers of big cities. Helicopters act as taxis, taking people to landing spots in cities and towns. A big building in New York has a heliport on its roof.

One very small whirlybird is called a gyrocopter. A pilot can buy a gyrocopter kit and build one himself. Then he can run it along a road like a scooter, or take off and fly cross-country. Some people attach the gyrocopter's rotor to a small boat. A big speed-boat then tows it over the water. Soon the copter boat takes off and flies along at the end of its rope high above the lake or stream.

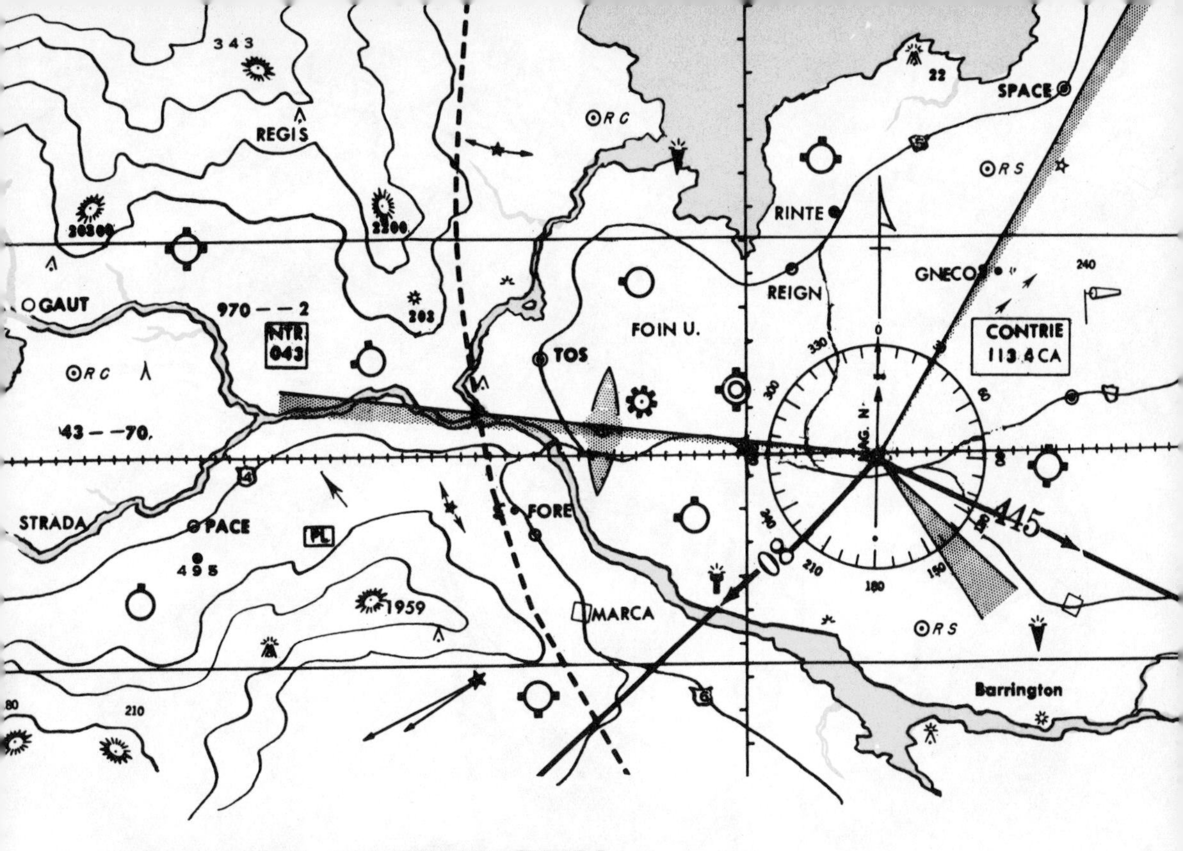

AIRWAYS IN THE SKY

The Wright brothers flew their first planes only a little way. But inventors kept making improvements, and after a while they could travel for miles cross-country. This meant that pilots had to know exactly where they were going. They needed maps, specially made for use in the air.

Map-making has always been the job of men in the United States Coast and Geodetic Survey. So they went to work. Now they have made maps called aeronautical charts for the whole country. The charts show where rivers flow, where railroads run, where there are highways and every other important landmark. They give the heights of mountains and the location of beacon lights that are like road markers. They show the airways, which are the best paths through the air for pilots to follow.

LOS ANGELES
CLOVER
N
34 02
118 20
MUNICIPAL
4

Some cities have air markers on top of buildings or water towers or gas tanks. The one in the picture gives the name of the city with an arrow pointing straight north. The figures above and below this arrow tell the exact location on the map. The fatter arrows point to the nearest airports. Sometimes you can see this same kind of information painted on roads, too.

Traffic in the airways is something like traffic in different lanes on roads. Pilots keep to the right. They are told what lane to follow when they leave their airports, and they must fly so that there is a safe distance of at least several thousand feet between them and any other plane above, below or to the left. The highest lanes are for jet planes.

The Coast and Geodetic Survey has planes of its own and pilots to fly them. When new maps are to be made, a pilot and a photographer fly very high. A huge camera in the plane takes pictures of the earth through nine different lenses at once. From these special pictures, men can draw maps very quickly. Before there were planes, surveyors spent years walking over the land and measuring it with instruments they carried along. Today pilots and photographers are mapping parts of the world where no explorer has ever been able to go.

DO IT YOURSELF

Most aircraft are now built in huge factories. But people still love to build flying machines of their own. Many builders belong to a group called the Experimental Aircraft Association. Every year members of the association have a show. The best homemade craft wins a prize.

According to the rules, a show plane must be small enough to fit into an ordinary garage. It must be inexpensive and easy and safe to fly. The owner can bring it to the show either by trailer or under its own power.

One kind of experimental craft is a cross between a plane and an automobile. When it travels along the road, its wing folds down on either side like a beetle's wings. When the pilot wants to take off, he unfolds the wing and uses the road for a runway — if there is no traffic.

Experimental planes must have special licenses.

SMOKE JUMPERS

Many kinds of aircraft help to put out fires and save our forests. The fires often start when lightening strikes in the wilderness, far from the nearest foot trail. Men with packs and tools on their backs might have to walk four or five days before they could reach the spot. Meanwhile the blaze could destroy vast amounts of timber. That often did happen — until planes and men with parachutes came along. Now this is how they work:

A patrol plane takes off from the airstrip near the Ranger Station in a high mountain valley. Soon it is high above the slopes, flying a course worked out in advance. A wisp of smoke appears. The pilot circles above it. Sure enough he sees a small fire burning. He marks the exact spot on a map, then he calls a special Ranger Station by radio.

Immediately another pilot warms up a big transport plane. A crew of husky young men climb in, and they're off with no waste time. The men wear football helmets and white cover-alls that have foam rubber pads on knees, hips and elbows. Each has two parachutes — one on his back and a spare on his chest to use if the other doesn't open.

These are the smoke jumpers — smokies — who dive into the forests to fight fire. As their transport bounces in the rough mountain air, every smokie inspects his own parachute pack. Then he inspects the pack on the jumper nearest him. All the straps and fastenings must be tight.

One man in the crew is called the spotter. He is a good judge of distance and he tells the pilot how to fly in over the area. Before he lets anyone jump, he drops a small parachute and watches how far it drifts in the wind. Now he can tell very accurately when the men must jump in order to land in a good spot. The spotter gives a signal. One after another the smokies step out of the door in the side of the plane. Crack, crack, like shots from a gun, their chutes open.

A smokie guides his parachute by pulling on lines that make it drift one way or another. He can make it drop him faster or slower. Usually he aims for the top of a tree. He knows that that's the softest place to land. Smoke jumpers call treetops "feathers."

Dangling forty or fifty feet in the air, a smoke jumper calmly gets out of the parachute harness, takes out a nylon rope, and slides down to the ground. There he stretches out a ribbon of bright yellow crepe paper. This tells the pilot that he has landed safely.

Now the pilot flies back over the same spot. Out go parachutes carrying all kinds of fire-fighting tools and a portable radio station. Five minutes after the smoke jumpers leave the plane, they are at work fighting the fire.

If the fire is big and they have to stay a long time, food comes down by parachute.

In some forests smoke jumpers go to the fire in smaller planes that carry only two or three at a time. Several small planes can scatter men over a wide area more quickly than one big transport can. The transport follows them with extra equipment.

HELIJUMPERS

In some parts of California helicopters carry smokies to fires. When they jump from a copter, they don't need parachutes. The copter just hovers, a few feet above the ground, and the men hop out.

Most forests have helicopters as well as transport planes and patrol planes. The copters can rescue men who get caught in a place surrounded by fire. They bring out anyone who is injured. And when the fire is over they taxi the men home. Before there were helicopters, smokies had to walk all the way out after a fire — and it was often a very long way.

WATER BOMBERS

By accident some test pilots discovered a new way of fire fighting. They were testing a brand new passenger plane, but it was filled with huge tanks of water instead of people. Something went wrong, and they dumped the water. A strip of land a mile long got drenched. This gave Forest Rangers the idea that they might be able to douse fires with water and with chemicals.

Old bombing planes have now been turned into lifesavers for forests. Some of them carry hundreds of gallons of water. Others carry a mixture of water and stuff called borate that smothers flames. In one forest the Rangers put out fires with a chemical that is also a plant food. It helps new trees to grow quickly, so they can take the place of the ones that were burned.

When a bomber goes out, a small patrol plane usually flies bird-dog. That is, the patrol pilot scouts the burning forest, then flies along close to the bomber and radios the crew when it is time to drop their load on the flames.

In Canada the water bombers are very big old flying boats that used to belong to the United States Navy. The bomber's tank can be filled in a few seconds. The pilot just comes down on a lake and opens up a special water scoop in the belly of the flying boat. As he skims along on the surface of the lake, the scoop takes water into the tank. Without stopping, the pilot climbs again and heads back to the fire.

BEACONS AND TOWERS

Planes that travel long distances have wonderful instruments to help the pilot fly safely at night or high over the clouds where no land can be seen. The most important help is radio. Special radio signals sent out from government stations tell pilots where they are and what direction they are flying.

Aids for pilots got their start when the Post Office began airmail service more than forty years ago. Fast mail had to travel by night as well as by day. So the government placed lighted beacons along the routes that pilots followed. Even bonfires were used at first to mark the airways.

Modern airports have many complicated inventions to help pilots land. A tall building at one side of the airport is the control tower. A man in the tower talks to pilots by radio. He tells them how to keep out of the way of other planes. He gives them orders about how and when to land.

When a pilot wants to land, he calls the control tower. Then he and the man in the tower begin to talk in a kind of special

language. The pilot first gives the name of his plane and its license number. He will say something like this:

"Beechcraft five-niner-Bravo."

Beechcraft is the type of plane. *Five-niner-Bravo* means 59B.

Numbers and letters are given in this strange way in order to avoid mistakes. *Nine* can be confused with *five* if the speaker is in a hurry or doesn't pronounce clearly. The letter *B* often sounds like *V*. Pilots have worked out a whole alphabet that goes like this:

A—Alfa
B—Bravo
C—Charlie
D—Delta
E—Echo
F—Foxtrot
G—Golf
H—Hotel
I —India
J—Juliett
K—Kilo (pronounced Key-low)
L—Lima (pronounced Lee-mah)
M—Mike
N—November
O—Oscar
P—Papa
Q—Quebec (pronounced Keh-bek)
R—Romeo
S—Sierra
T—Tango
U—Uniform
V—Victor
W—Whiskey
X—X-ray
Y—Yankee
Z—Zulu

When the man in the control tower tells the pilot where to land, he will say something like this: "Beechcraft five-niner-Bravo cleared to enter traffic pattern runway one four. Over."

Over means that the control tower has finished talking but expects the pilot to answer. The pilot then says, "Beechcraft five-niner-Bravo, Roger. Out." This means he understands and has nothing more to say.

The first time a pilot hears this kind of talk, it may sound very confusing. If he wants to get used to the strange words before he actually has to land at a big busy airport, he can buy records that give him lessons and practice in flight lingo.

If many planes are coming toward a busy airport, the man in the control tower says he "stacks them up." This means he tells the pilots to fly around and around, each one at a different altitude, so they can't bump. Then he orders them one by one to land.

If the weather turns bad before a pilot reaches an airport, it is sometimes necessary to "talk him down" through clouds and fog. Some airports have radar equipment, which helps the man on the ground to judge where a plane is, even though he can't see it. He talks to the pilot and tells him just what turns to make and how to head for the runway and when to set the plane down.

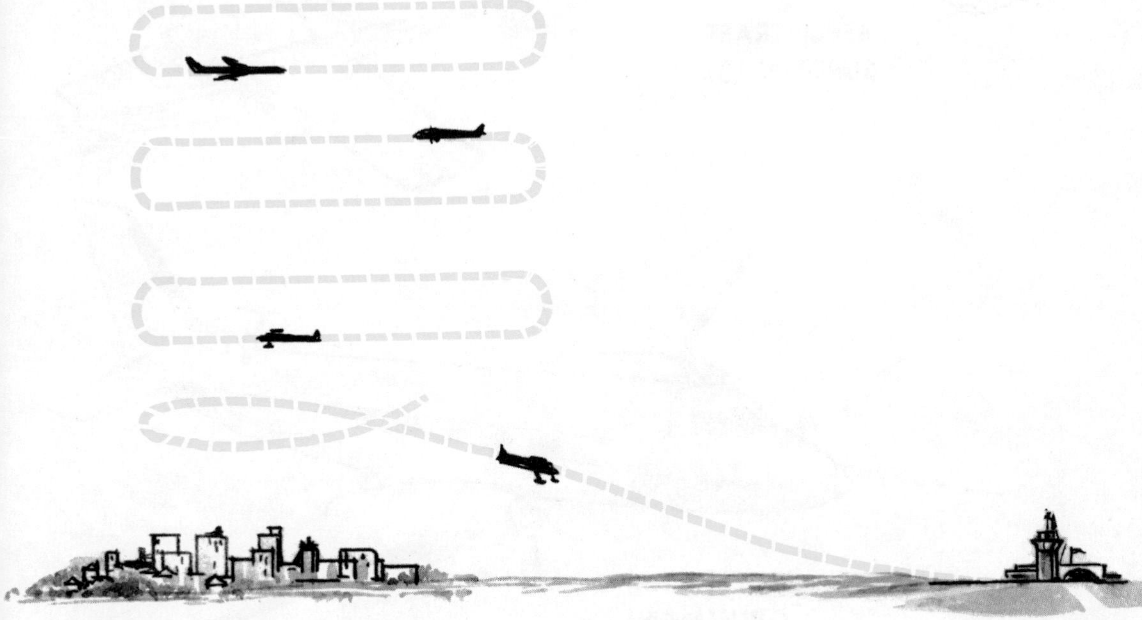

EXECUTIVE PLANES

The control tower men at a big airport help all kinds of pilots to land. Some of the pilots work for big companies that have planes just for company business. These are called executive planes because the officers or executives of the business use them most.

Some of these planes are very fancy. Some have desks so that people can work as they fly. A few movie and television stars travel in their own executive planes, and they sometimes act as pilots or co-pilots.

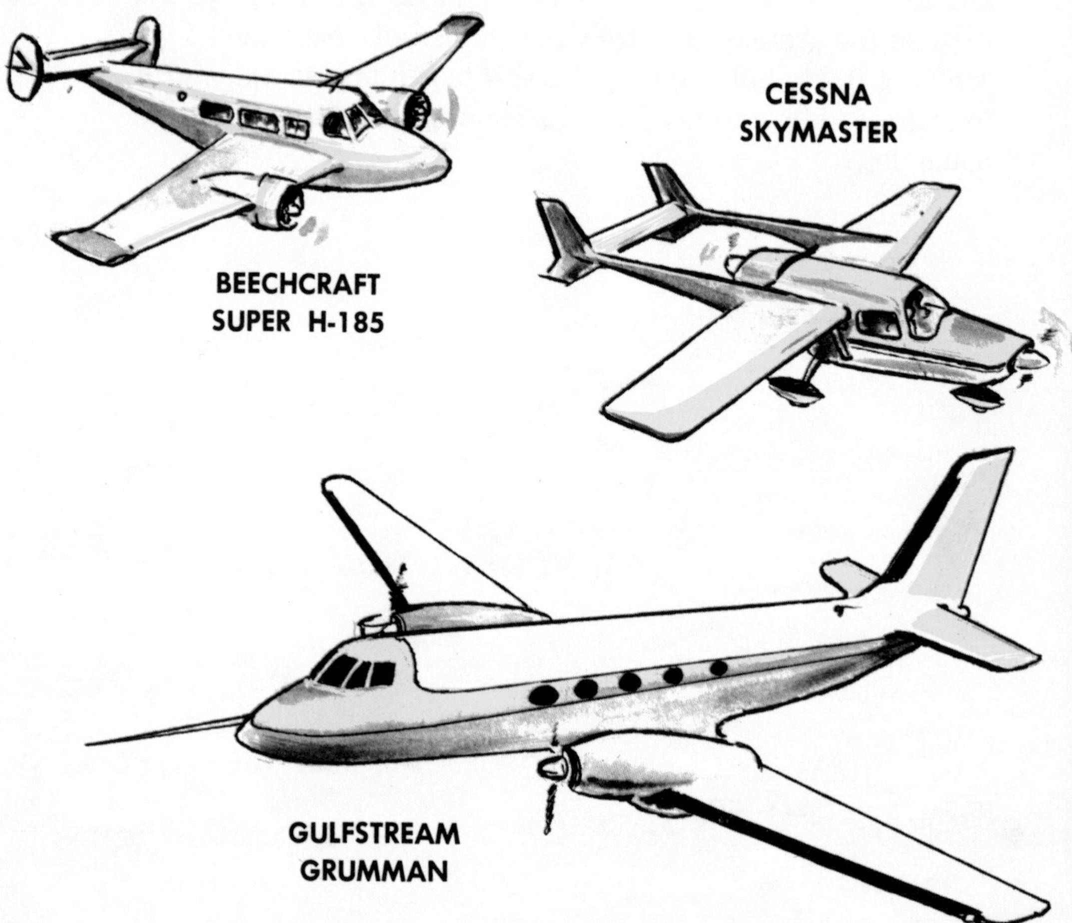

ALL KINDS OF CARGO

Big cargo planes carry freight everywhere in the world. The pilot and the crew of a cargo plane are always ready for surprising things to come aboard. Once the crew turned the plane into a flying barn for some prize bulls going to South America. The men didn't mind, until one bull got loose and began to lick the pilot's neck. Luckily that was all that happened, and the bull went back to his stall after a while.

Race horses often fly across the ocean. They get seasick on a ship, but in a plane they feel fine. A groom always goes along to take care of a horse. Sometimes he brings a monkey or a cat or a goat to keep the horse from being lonely.

One cargo plane left New York with heavy parts for a ship that had broken down halfway around the world in Singapore. Then it flew back, loaded with six baby elephants, 116 monkeys, four apes, four leopards, a couple of tigers, and a big python. On the way home the crew had to feed the animals — except the python. He had eaten seven chickens before starting, and he slept all the way to New York!

A tiger is likely to frighten other animals in a plane. They get nervous as soon as they catch a whiff of its scent. So the tiger's cage is put in the tail of the plane, next to a fan that blows the scent out. Nervous monkeys don't cause any great problems, but an upset elephant can be troublesome, even dangerous. If it breaks loose and rushes around, its shifting weight may unbalance the plane. Luckily an elephant stays calm if it has a chicken in its pen. One airline keeps a whole flock of hens called Elephant Girls that go along to comfort the big passengers.

At one English airport there is an animal hotel where any kind of creature can get proper food and a place to rest. The hotel has cold rooms for polar bears and hot ones for jungle animals.

Of course cargo planes carry other things besides animals. They haul any kind of freight, and especially anything that needs to be delivered quickly. Flowers and movie film, fresh vegetables and emergency medicines all travel by plane. Air mail goes either by cargo plane or in the cargo room of regular passenger planes.

"FLYING ZEBRA"

Many zoo animals come from Africa where they live in large herds in national parks. These herds have been getting smaller, and there is danger that some kinds of animals may die out entirely. Of course people in Africa do not want that to happen, so they have asked scientists for help. First, the scientists decided, they had to find out just how many wild animals really did live in certain places. Flying low over the herds in a plane, they counted creatures of many kinds. The job was hard, but after a while the men became very skillful at it. The plane they used had black and white zebra stripes painted all over it. If the pilot had to make an emergency landing, searchers could see the stripes easily and send out a rescue party.

MAKE-BELIEVE FLYING

Pilots who fly the very big planes have to go to school and study for several months. Look at the picture and you'll see how many instruments a pilot must use and understand.

A man needs a great deal of practice in a cockpit like this. But he doesn't have to be in the air all the time he is learning. A machine can teach him many things without ever leaving the ground. The machine is called a simulator. That means it just pretends to fly.

The pilot, co-pilot and other crew members climb into the training cockpit, which is exactly like a real one. It has all the instruments, and they are connected with machinery in the room where the simulator is set up.

The pilot puts on earphones. Instructions come through to him from a make-believe control tower operator, just as they would if he were really ready to take off from an airport. He answers and pushes the throttle forward. The instruments in front of him show just what they would show in a real take-off. The controls feel just as they do when air is rushing over the wings and tail.

The make-believe plane seems to climb. The instruments show when the pilot makes a turn. Even the compass pretends.

After a while the teacher gives the crew a surprise. He makes it seem that one of the engines is quitting. The controls shake as they would in a real emergency. The teacher can put the plane through everything bad that can really happen on a flight. When the crew members step out after the lesson, they feel as if they have been through terrible danger. And all the while the simulator hasn't moved an inch!

Some simulators have a special way of training the pilot to take off and land. He sits in the cockpit and looks out through the windshield, and there in front of him seems to be an actual airport. It is really a sort of television screen with a movie being shown on it. As the pilot uses his controls, he sees on the screen what he would see if the plane were moving. The picture seems very real, and it teaches him what to expect when he is actually piloting a plane.

A trainer like this costs almost as much as the very expensive airplane it imitates — more than two million dollars.

JETLINER

The men who pilot the huge jetliners must go to special schools, no matter how long they have been flying. Most of them have been pilots on other big airliners for many years. A jet is different from other planes. It is bigger and it goes much faster. Men have to spend time just getting used to it. After they have been trained in a simulator, they practice in real jets. At last they are ready to take examinations. If they pass, they can fly the jets. But the pilots still have to take several tests every year after that. If they fail even one, they must go back to flying easier planes.

Long before a jetliner takes off, men are busy getting it ready. Mechanics and inspectors go over all its working parts. They check everything and fix whatever is worn out or broken. These men belong to the ground crew. There are twenty or thirty of them, and they may spend the whole night preparing the plane to leave in the morning. When they finish, fuel is put in the tanks, and the big ship is ready for another inspection. This time the flight crew's engineer goes over everything.

He calls it a walk-around check. He also makes sure the fuel tanks really have been filled.

Meantime the pilot, who is called the Captain, has also been checking. He has decided how far he will have to run along the ground in order to get the ship into the air with its load. On a hot summer day he needs a much longer run than in cool weather.

The Captain has made a flight plan, too. If for any reason at all he thinks the flight should not be made, he can call it off. He has the last word, always.

Five men will work in the cockpit while the jet speeds along. Besides the Captain and the flight engineer, there will be a first officer, a second officer and a navigator. The navigator knows how to look at the stars and figure out where the plane is, just in case its radio and other instruments stop working.

These men check, double-check, watch and do everything else you can think of to make the flight safe. On some jets the Captain and the first officer eat their meals one hour apart. If by any chance the food should make the first man sick, the second would go hungry and fly the plane!

IN THE CABIN

Suppose you are going to take a trip across the ocean in a jetliner. First you and your baggage get weighed on scales at the airport. The pilot must know just how big a load his plane will have. Then you go to a special waiting-room-on-wheels. There you can sit in soft chairs and look out through picture windows. When it is time for you to board your plane, the whole waiting-room rolls away from the main building to the jet on the runway. When it stops, a gangplank pokes itself out. You walk across it into the plane's cabin.

A stewardess in uniform meets you at the door. She looks at your ticket, checks it against the list of passengers that she holds in her hand, and tells you which seat is yours. You may be surprised later to find that she knows your name, but she has been trained to remember which passenger is which.

When the plane is ready to take off, she or one of the other stewardesses makes sure that everybody is sitting down, with his seat belt properly fastened. The belt keeps you from being thrown against the seat ahead of you if the plane should have a rough take-off or landing.

Now the cabin door is locked, and the waiting-room wheels itself away. In a moment you hear a voice on the loudspeaker saying, "This is your Captain."

The Captain gives a little talk about the trip, and then you're off. Before you know it, you're streaking along at 600 miles an hour almost five miles above the earth.

You unbuckle your seat belt. The stewardess tells you she has magazines and comics and games for you to play. She'll bring you a non-skid checkerboard, if you like, with men that can't slip off the board.

At dinnertime, she brings you a tray of hot food. It came aboard at the airport, and she heated it in an electric oven in the plane's kitchen, which is called the galley.

The stewardess has many things to make passengers comfortable — a pillow, pills that keep you from getting airsick, even a supply of diapers for small babies. Every once in a while she gives you news about the flight — how far you've gone, how high in the air you're travelling, what time it is at home.

On some airliners you can sleep overnight in a berth, just the way you do in a Pullman car on a train. But a jetliner goes so fast that there isn't time for you to eat and go to bed and get up again before the end of the flight. The whole trip from the United States to Europe takes less than eight hours.

The older, slower airliners are called props because they have propellers. They are also called piston planes because their engines have pistons. The piston engine in an airplane works somewhat like the one in an automobile. But instead of turning wheels it turns a propeller. Propellers pull the plane through the air.

A prop plane moves forward when the propeller thrusts air backward. A jet plane, too, moves forward when its engines thrust air and other gases backward. But a jet has neither props nor pistons. This is how it works: First a large quantity of air is sucked into the front of the engine. There it is compressed — that is, the particles of air are squeezed tightly together. Now part of the compressed air is combined with some fuel, which burns and produces very hot gases. These hot gases, along with the rest of the compressed air, can escape through the opening at the back of the engine. Since nothing is squeezing them now, they expand and rush out with great speed. This great backward rush produces the thrust that is needed, and the plane moves forward.

The wings of jet planes are very special. They are attached to the fuselage at an angle so that they look as if the tips had been pushed backward. These *swept* wings allow the jets to fly much faster than straight wings.

When a jet takes off, its engines sound very noisy to people on the ground. But inside the cabin, you hear nothing but a low roar that decreases as you rise. The huge liner cuts through the air like a fish through water. It's the smoothest flying machine in the world.

WHAT'S TO COME

Many experts believe that jetliners will soon be flying three times as fast as they fly today. Such planes could be built right now. But no one knows whether they would really be useful and practical and safe. Some people doubt that men need to be in that much of a hurry.

In the future small planes will probably be safer and easier to fly than they are now. They will have new automatic instruments to help the pilot. Perhaps some light planes will take off and land straight up and down like helicopters, then fly forward with fixed wings. That kind of aircraft has already been built for the army. It is called a VTOL, which means *V*ertical *T*ake-*O*ff and *L*anding.

Flying is only a little more than sixty years old, but it has already become a very important part of our lives. Planes have been doing more and more of the work of the world. They will have even more important jobs to do in the future.

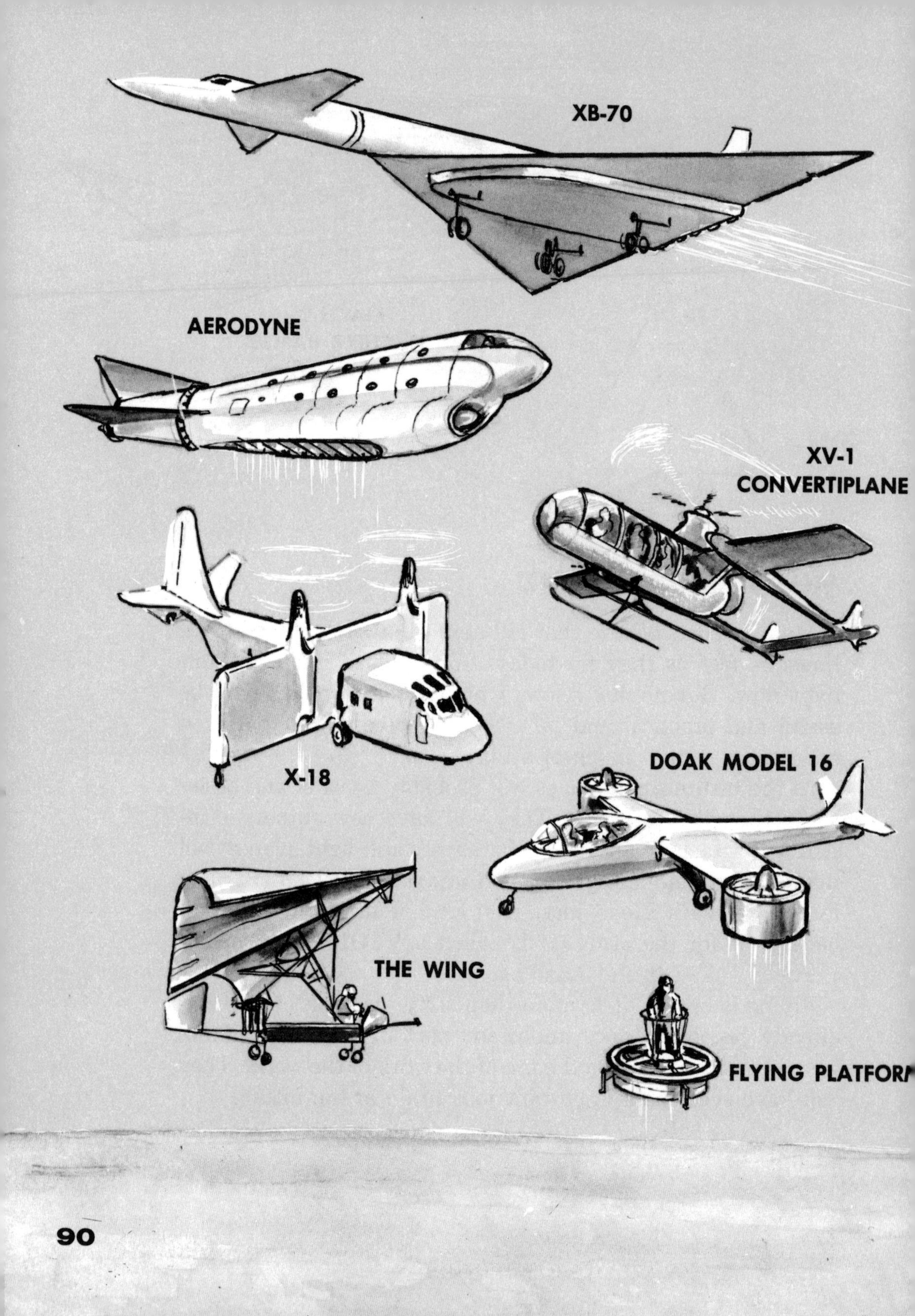
XB-70
AERODYNE
XV-1
CONVERTIPLANE
X-18
DOAK MODEL 16
THE WING
FLYING PLATFOR

AVIATION TALK

Here are some special words that you haven't found earlier in the book:

AUX TANK — short for auxiliary tank, one that carries extra gasoline for long flights.

JET JOCK — the pilot of a jet plane.

LITTLE BLACK BOX — instruments that work automatically so that the plane can fly even when the pilot leaves the controls for a little while.

MONKEY — a mechanic at an airport is sometimes nicknamed a *monkey*.

PANTS — when a plane does not have retractable landing gear, its wheels sometimes have covers that pilots call *pants*.

POD — the part of a jet plane that carries the engine. It looks something like a seed pod.

PORPOISING — some planes are hard to fly in a straight, level path at certain speeds. Instead they move slowly up, then slowly down, like a dolphin in the sea. The motion is called *porpoising*.

SPOILERS — plates attached to a jet's wing. The pilot can move them so that they *spoil* the wing's lifting power and so help the brakes to stop the plane when it lands.

SQUAWK SHEET—when a mechanic and an inspector go over a plane, they make out a list of things that need fixing. This is a *squawk sheet*.

INDEX

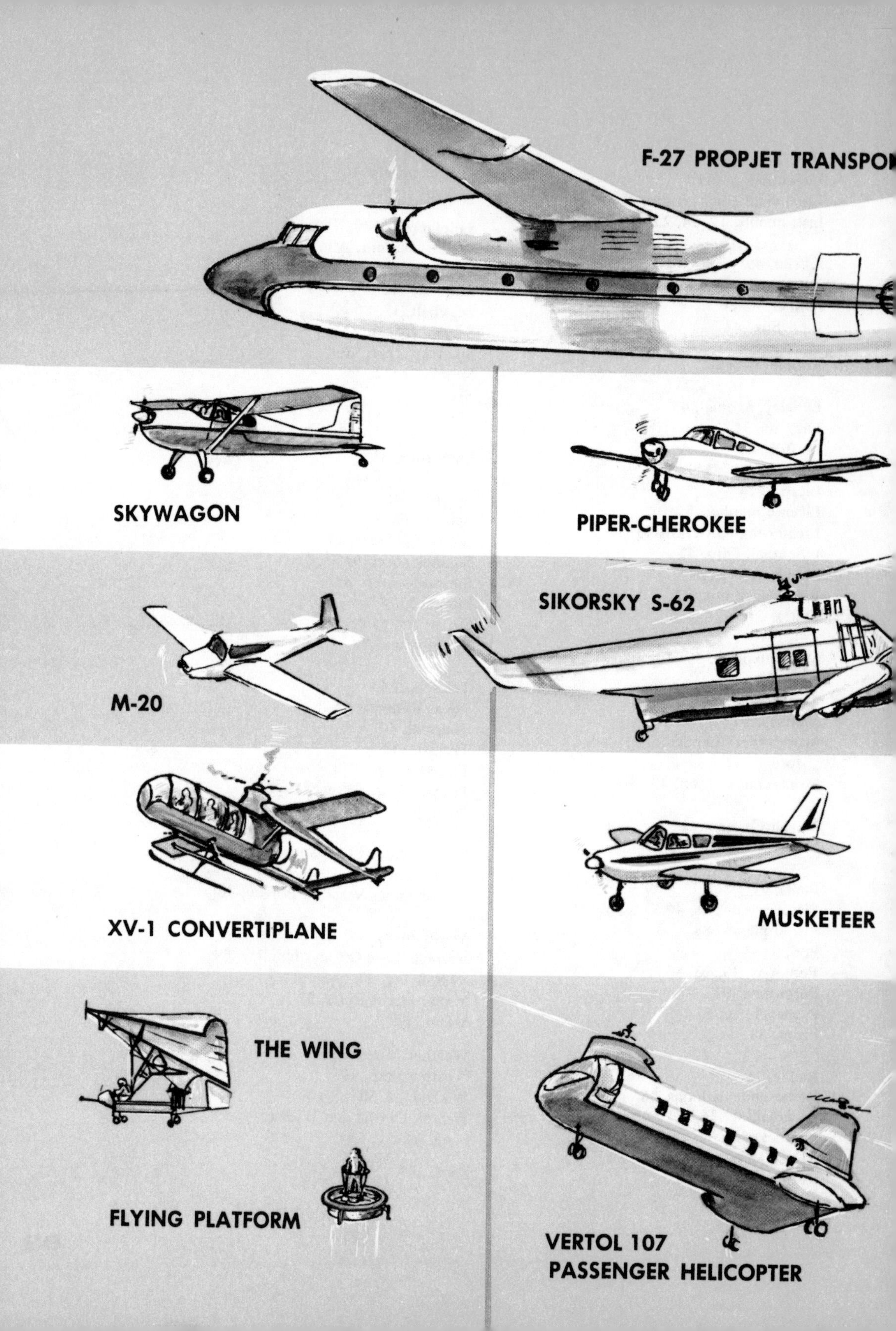
F-27 PROPJET TRANSPO
SKYWAGON
PIPER-CHEROKEE
SIKORSKY S-62
M-20
XV-1 CONVERTIPLANE
MUSKETEER
THE WING
FLYING PLATFORM
VERTOL 107
PASSENGER HELICOPTER

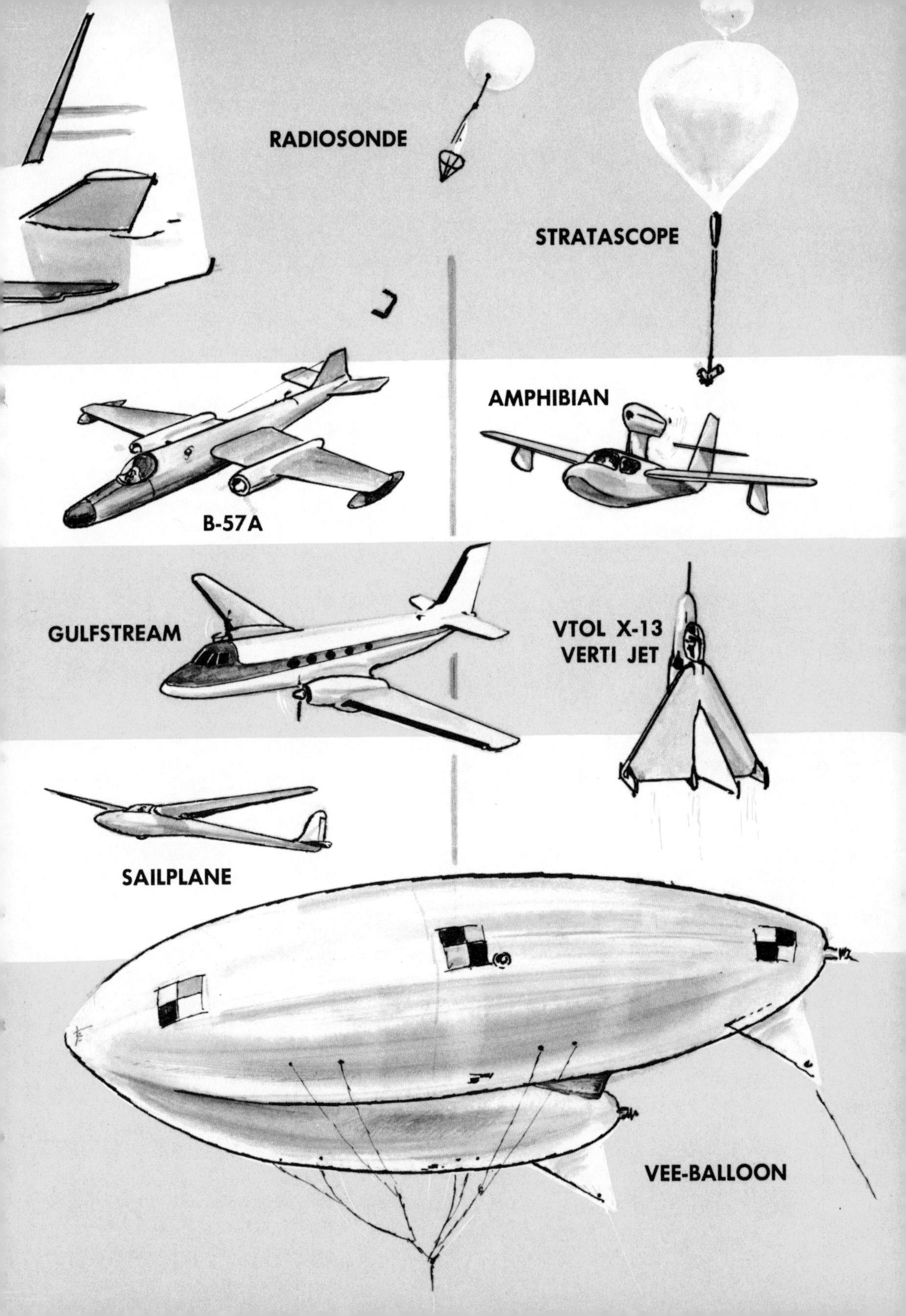
RADIOSONDE
STRATASCOPE
AMPHIBIAN
B-57A
GULFSTREAM
VTOL X-13
VERTI JET
SAILPLANE
VEE-BALLOON